Railway Track Diagrams
Book 2: Eastern
Editor: Gerald Jacobs

CW00401902

Preface to the Third Edition

Quail Track Diagrams have been published since 1988 and provide a reference to Enthusiasts and Industry alike. They contain information which may exist elsewhere and in other forms but are unique in making it all available in one easily portable volume.

The idea was not new at the time but only when Gerald Jacobs, with his historical sources collected over 40 years with British Railways, joined forces with John Yonge of the Quail Map Co as cartographer and publisher did the principle find two people with the knowledge and the attention to detail to put it into full and effective practice. The result of this collaboration has become the standard reference work for a wide range of users from train staff and infrastructure managers to railway enthusiast and modellers.

In 2004, TRACKmaps took over the publication of these volumes and embarked on the digital conversion of the information as well as incorporating updates. The first volumes to be revised were Books 3 and 4, both published in 2005.

This book, Book 2 in the series, was last updated in 1998 and represents a tremendous amount of work in catching up the intervening years. The Publisher believes it will be as well received as the other recent updates.

September 2006

Introduction

The Track Diagrams in this book cover the lines forming most of LNE Territory of Network Rail, also parts of LNW and South Eastern, together with a selected number of private railways and industrial layouts. They are, in general, up to date as at September 2006.

Outside of Network Rail Territory, it is difficult, if not impossible, to determine who is responsible for infrastructure, direct enquiry often being unsuccessful. Consequently, what is shown may be dated and lack authentication.

However, records are wonderful things which can both inform and confuse. This is evident on the UK Railway Network, built up as it has been over more than 180 years, managed as individual companies, as a nationalised industry and now as individual train operating companies with a single infrastructure owner. It has grown, stagnated, declined and grown again more than once within that time and many persons have produced records and maps at different times for different parts, both within the industry and outside. Many record systems compete for information or act in a complementary manner to each other. The Track Diagrams attempt to collate these diverse sources into one publication but, even so, space precludes the inclusion of much detail including, for example, signals. These may be the subject of later publications.

Track Diagrams also try to put down a standard where discrepancies occur. Mileages are typical, often varying between different official records but, in general, those given in Sectional Appendix have been used. Station mileages are usually taken from the mid-point of the platforms or, in the case of a terminus, the buffer stops. The Railway is continually changing and, because of its diverse nature and varied history, discrepancies often arise between seeming accurate sources. In such circumstances, the Editor's judgement is applied.

Acknowledgments

There are many contributors to the information in this publication; some significant providing layouts, site checking or proofing details and some in a small way giving personal observations, answering individual questions or giving access to engineering drawings and construction diagrams. The assistance of all is gratefully acknowledged, especially persons at Network Rail (including its predecessors), at EWS Railways, at London Underground, together with Iain Scotchman, Michael Oakley, Eddie Scarlett and Charles Allenby.

The Editor is also indebted to Peter Scott for details of certain private and preserved layouts (see also Peter Scott's website http://web.ukonline.co.uk/pe.scott). Other acknowledgments are due to the Branch Line Society, the Railway Correspondence & Travel Society and many other correspondents, other railway societies and also representatives of the other private and preserved systems featured.

The digital production of this book could not have proceeded without the efforts of the team at ESR Cartography Ltd but special thanks must also be given to two people; firstly, to John Yonge, the originator of the track diagram artwork, whose cartography provided a sound basis of the maps in the book; and, secondly, to Elvina Jacobs for her forbearance and continuous support given throughout the Editor's long and arduous task.

Gerald Jacobs

1st Edition 1994 (reprint)
2nd Edition 1998
3rd Edition 2006

ISBN 0-9549866-2-8

Published by TRACKmaps
Little Court, Upper South Wraxall, Bradford on Avon BA15 2SE (Tel: 0845 300 1370 Fax: 0845 300 1375)
Web: www.trackmaps.co.uk Email: sales@trackmaps.co.uk

Edited by Gerald Jacobs

Original Cartography by John Yonge

Digital Conversion & Design by ESR Cartography Ltd
Maidenhead, Berkshire SL6 8BR

Printed by Brightsea Press,
Exeter EX5 2UL

KEY

———	Running Line
———	Siding
———	Electrified overhead
———	Electrified 3rd rail
———	Electrified 3rd rail (Underail contact, DLR)
———	Electrified 4th rail (LU)
··········	Electrified, overhead & Conductor rail

A broken line indicates 'in situ' but out of use, proposed or under construction.

——●——	Line obstructed
——○——	Line out of use
——⋮——	Change of Signalling mandate
LNW ╫ LNE	Network Rail Territory boundary
Doncaster │ York (D) │ (Y)	Signal Box / centre area limits (Within an area, plates on automatic signals may reflect actual line description)
—┤---├—	Tunnel
≈	Bridge under Rail or Viaduct
—X—	Selected Motorway / Trunk Road bridges over rail
—┼—	Network Rail operated level crossing
—┆—	User-worked crossing with Telephone
◄——►	Track signalled in both directions (a double arrow indicates normal direction of travel) (On single lines 'DN' indicates down direction)
—⋈—	Private siding boundary, often marked by a gate
———┐	Sand Drag
—◯—	Turntable
··············	Gantry Rails (Freightliner Terminal)
wwwwwwww	Wall / Bank
——▲——	Hot Axle Box Detector (HABD), Wheel Impact Load Detector (WILD) or Wheelchex Device

ECM	ELR-Engineer's Line Reference (Prefix and suffix numbers indicate sub-divisions and their boundaries)
[LN 101]	Line of Route Code
│ 93	Whole mileposts, shown on the appropriate side of the line
│ 32	Whole kilometre posts
81.3⌉	End of mileage run
113.76 / 105.70 COM	Lineside mileage change
3	Platform with number (May be supplemented by sub-divisions. e.g. (a), (b), (c), 'N' or North etc)
⑦	Indicates number of carriages per platform (approx 20m lengths)
⌝⌞	Provisional proposed platform
▭	Former Royal Mail platform
▭	Platform out of use
⌂	Other feature (labelled)
▨	Loading bank
Doncaster (D) ⊠	Signal Box or Signalling Centre, with code (underlined text relates to SB or SC)
▧	Control Panel
⊠	Gate Box
▫⊙	Ground Frame/Ground Switch Panel or Shunting Frame. Ⓢ Indicates 'Shut in' facility
⊛	Radio electronic token block / Token exchange point
¶	Proposed closure
◯	Water tower
∧	Summit, height in feet
(Three Counties) ●	Indicates a former Jn, Station or Signal Box
86.34 *(Not italic if Station mileage)*	Distance in Miles and chains from specified zero 1 Mile = 1760 yards / 1.6km 80 chains = 1 Mile 1 chain = 22 yards / 20.11m
57.60 km	Distance in Kilometres

Guide references are given to pre-nationalisation, pre-grouping and sometimes pioneer railways e.g. LMS : LNW (London & Birmingham)

Traditional Line Descriptions may be quoted, e.g. CROUCH VALLEY LINE

London Underground Signalling

LU signalling is controlled at some places by local Signal Cabins, or for a long part or the whole of some lines by Signal Control Centres.
Because of different cables, LU has Interlocking Machines operated by air motors (or comparable equipment) in unmanned rooms near points, except where a local cabin has an interlocking lever frame.
IMR's (and equivalent rooms) are included in these maps, but purely Relay Rooms (and their equivalents) are not.
IMR's bear the name of the adjacent station unless otherwise noted: (e) indicates location at the end of the platform, (m) in the middle of the platform.

ⓙⓙ	Unmanned Interlocking Machine (or comparable equipment) Room, with code	ⓙⓟ	Interlocking within manned cabin, with code(s), controlled
Ⓦⓟ	Interlocking inside former cabin, with code	JP │ JJ	Code area boundaries (where not separated by a long stretch of plain track(s))

Publisher's Note

Every effort has been made by the editor to ensure the accuracy of the information in the book is as correct as possible at the time of going to press. Notwithstanding, the Publishers welcome corrections, updates or suggestions for application to future editions

GENERAL ABBREVIATIONS

AA	Acid Application	FP	Fuelling Point or Footpath	PW	Permanent Way
ABP	Associated British Ports	ft	Feet	Qy	Query concerning distances etc, unresolved
AC	Alternating Current	GB	Gate Box	REC	Reception
ARR	Arrival	GC	Gantry Crane	RETB	Radio Electronic Token Block
ASC	Area Signalling Centre i/c IECC, Power Box	GDS	Goods	REV	Reversing or Reversible line
bdy	boundary	GF	Ground Frame	RR	Run-Round
BCH	Branch	GL	Goods Loop	S	South
BR	British Rail	GS	Goods Shed	S & T	Signal & Telegraph
CCTV	Closed Circuit Television	GSP	Ground Switch Panel	SB	Signal Box or Southbound
CET	Controlled Emission Toilet Discharge	H	Headshunt	SC	Signalling Centre
CL	Crossing Loop on Single Line	HABD	Hot Axle Box Detector	SCC	Signalling Control Centre
COM	Change of Mileage	HH	Hopper House	Sdg(s)	Siding(s)
CR	Cripple Siding	HST	High Speed Train	SD	Sand Drag
CW	Carriage Washer	IECC	Intergrated Electronic Control Centre	SF	Shunting Frame
C&W	Carriage & Wagon	Jn	Junction	SIMBIDS	Simplified Bi-Directional Signalling
D	Connections Disconnected	Jt	Joint	SN	Shunt Neck
DA	Down Avoiding	km	kilometres	SP	Switch Panel
DC	Direct Current	L	Wheel Lathe	SS	Shunt Spur
DE	Down Electric	LC	Level Crossing (manned, automatic or open)	TA	Tamper siding
DED	Diesel Electric Depot	LHS	Locomotive Holding Siding	TB	Turnback Siding
DEP	Departure	LP	Loop	TEP	Token Exchange Point
DF	Down Fast	LPG	Liquified petroleum gas	TL	Traffic Lights
DG	Down Goods	LS	Locomotive Shed	TMD	Traction Maintenance Depot
DGL	Down Goods Loop	LW	Locomotive Washer	T&RSMD	Traction & Rolling Stock Maintenance Depot
DL	Down Loop	M	Middle	U&D	Up & Down
DM	Down Main	M ch	Miles and Chains	UA	Up Avoiding
DMD	Diesel Maintenance Depot	M&EE	Mechanical & Electrical Engineer	UE	Up Electric
DMUD	Diesel Multiple Unit Depot	MGR	'Merry-go-round'	UF	Up Fast
DN	Down	MN	Main	UFN	Until Further Notice
DPL	Down Passenger Loop	MOD	Ministry of Defence	UG	Up Goods
DR	Down Relief	MU	Maintenance Unit	UGL	Up Goods Loop
DRS	Down Refuge Sidings	N	North	UH	Unloading Hopper
DS	Down Slow	n	not electrified	UL	Up Loop
DSB	Down Surburban	NB	Northbound	UM	Up Main
DT	Down Through	NIRU	Not in regular use	UPL	Up Passenger Loop
E	East	NR	Network Rail	UR	Up Relief
e	elecrified	OHC	Overhead Crane	URS	Up Refuge Siding
EB	Eastbound	OHLE	Overhead Line Equipment	US	Up Slow
EGF	Emergency Ground Frame	OOU	Out of Use	USB	Up Suburban
EMD	Electric Maintenance Depot	ONS	Overhead Neutral Section	UT	Up Through
EMUD	Electric Multiple Unit Depot	OTM	On-track Maintenance	V or Vdct	Viaduct
Engrs	Engineers' Sidings	P	Points padlocked	W	West
eol	End of Line	PAD	Prefabricated Assembly Depot	WB	Westbound or Weighbridge
ESP	Emergency Signalling Panel	PL	Passenger Loop	WD	War Department or Wheelchex Device
EWS	English Welsh & Scottish Railway Ltd	PS	Private Siding	WILD	Wheel Impact Load Detector
FA	Flushing Apron	PSB	Power Signal Box	yds	yards

SUPPLEMENTARY ABBREVIATIONS FOR THIS BOOK

Cal	former Caledonian Railway	LSW	former London and South Western Railway
CTRL	Channel Tunnel Rail Link	LT&S	former London, Tilbury & Southend Railway
EC	former Eastern Counties Railway	LUL	London Underground Limited
GC	former Great Central Railway	Met	former Metropolitan Railway
GE	former Great Eastern Railway	Mid	former Midland Railway
GN	former Great Northern Railway	NB	former North British Railway
GW	former Great Western Railway	NE	former North Eastern Railway
H&B	former Hull & Barnsley Railway	NL	former North London Railway
L&Y	former Lancashire & Yorkshire Railway	N&SWJn	former North and South Western Jn Railway
LMS	former London Midland and Scottish Railway	S	former Southern Railway
LNE	former London and North Eastern Railway	S&D	former Stockton & Darlington Railway
LNW	former London and North Western Railway	WL	former West London Joint Railway
LPTB	former London Passenger Transport Board	WLE	former West London Extension Joint Railway

LEVEL CROSSING ABBREVIATIONS

STANDARD	Supplementary	Description	STANDARD	Supplementary	Description
(ABCL) *		Automatic Barrier Crossing, Locally monitored		(MWLO)	Miniature Warning Lights at Open crossing
(AHBC) *		Automatic Half-Barrier Crossing	(OC)	(O) (OPEN)	Open Crossing (non-automatic), without barriers, gates or road traffic signals
(AOCL) *		Automatic Open Crossing, Locally monitored			
	(AOCR)	Automatic Open Crossing, Remotely monitored	(RC)		Remotely Controlled crossing with barriers
	(BW)	Bridle Way	(R/G)		User-worked crossing with Red and Green warning lights operated by approaching trains
(CCTV)		Manually controlled barrier crossing with Closed Circuit Television			
			(TMO)		Traincrew Operated crossing
	(FP (B)(G)(K)(W))	Footpath crossing (only shown if telephone provided) (B) Barriers, (G) Gates, (K) Kissing Gate, (W) Wickets		(TMOB)	Traincrew Operated Barrier
				(TMOG)	Traincrew Operated Gates
(MCB)	(MB)	Manually controlled Crossing with Barriers	(UWC)	(UWCP)	User-Worked Crossing of occupation, accommodation or bridleway status with telephone
	(MCBR)	Manually controlled Crossing with Barriers, Remotely controlled			
(MG)	(MCG)	Manually controlled Crossing with Gates		(UWB)	User-Worked Barriers
	(MGH)	Manned Gates, Hand worked		(UWCM)	User-Worked Crossing with miniature Red and Green warning lights
	(MGW)	Manned Gates with Wickets			
	(MSL (B)(F)(G))	Miniature Stop Light with (B) Barriers, (F) Footpath, (G) Gates		(UWG)	User-Worked Gates
	(MWL)	Miniature Warning Lights		(UWK)	User-Worked with Kissing Gates
	(MWLB)	Miniature Warning Lights with Barriers		(UWS)	User-Worked Stile
	(MWLF)	Miniature Warning Lights at user-worked Footpath		(UWW)	User-Worked Wickets
	(MWLG)	Miniature Warning Lights with Gates		(WL)	Barrow or Foot Crossing with White Light indicators

* (-X) shown after these abbreviations e.g. (AHBC-X) indicates that the crossing works automatically for movements in the wrong direction.

In some cases, the code of the controlling signal box may be shown e.g. (AHBC-X) (KS).

If no abbreviation is shown, the level crossing is either operated locally by a Signaller or Crossing Keeper, or privately but equipped with a telephone.

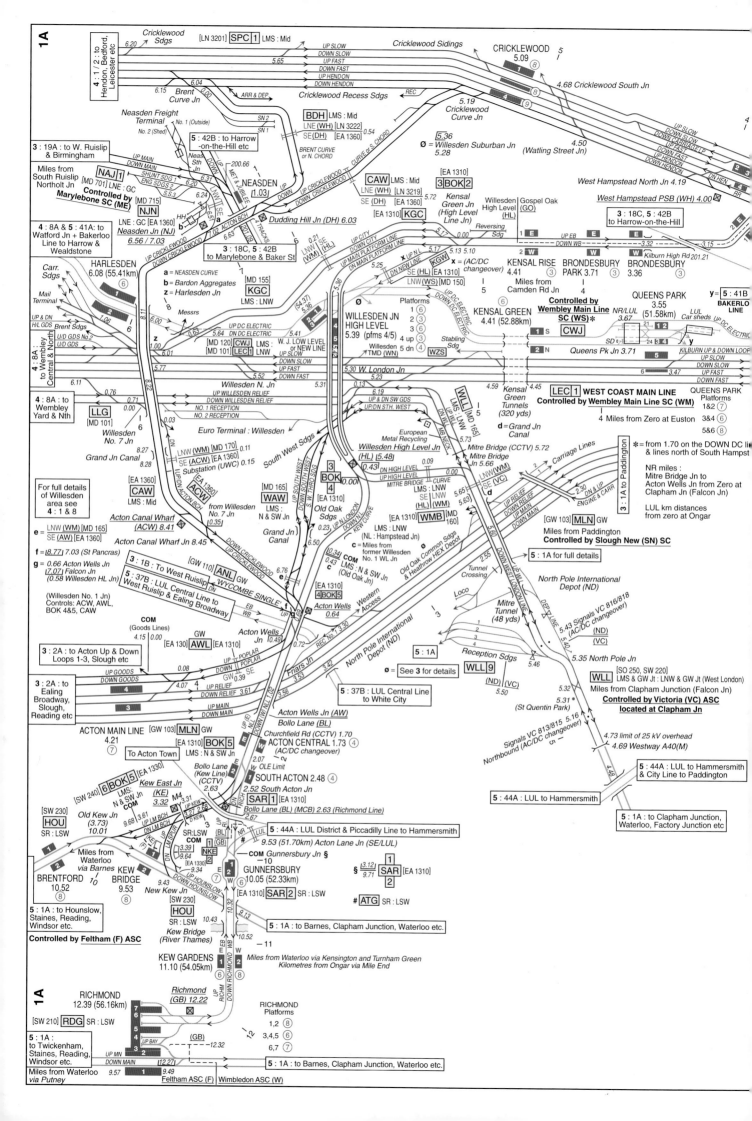

NORTH LONDON LINE • TOTTENHAM & HAMPSTEAD LINE

Hampstead Heath Tunnel
(1166 yds)
(NL : Hampstead Jn)

[EA 1310] BOK 2
LMS : LNW

1.63-1.56 Supported Cutting

1.63

FINCHLEY ROAD & FROGNAL
2.44
③

E W

UP MAIN (EB)
DOWN MAIN (WB)

E

Gospel Oak (GO)
1.12/0.00
-0.04

LNE & LMS Jt : GE & Mid Jt
Mortimer St Highgate
Vdct Road Vdct
0.23-26 0.28

Covered Way
(185yds)
0.43 0.52

[EA 1370] GOJ [EA 1370]
2 JRT TAH 1
[EA 1370]

LNE & LMS Jt :
GE & Mid Jt

UPPER HOLLOWAY
3.00 ⑥

DN T & H
UP T & H

GOSPEL OAK SPUR

0.58

DOWN SDG
DOWN T & H
RECEPTION LINE

D

1B

2.36
2.41 Covered Way
1.74 LUL Edgware Branch under

HAMPSTEAD HEATH
1.53 ③

1.15
Gospel Oak Jn

(HL) (GO)

Miles from Camden Road Jn

0.00
0.04 GOSPEL OAK
1.06

0.16
2.00 COM
0.18

2.12
2.15
2.17
2.21

T.N.C.Tnl 3 (103 yds)
T.N.C.Tnl 2 (70 yds)

2.27

2.36
2.42 Junction Rd Jn
2.38

LNE SE
(WH) (K)

2.55
Criple Sdg
GF

Upper Holloway (UH)
2.76

2 JRT 1
[LN 3210]

former Mortimer St Jn
LNE & LMS Jt : GE & Mid Jt
(Tottenham & Hampstead Jn)

Miles from St Pancras via Kentish Town

3

Belsize Slow Lines Tunnel (1 mile, 107 yds)

3.34

3.50
Finchley Road
3.32

Belsize Fast Lines Tunnel (1 mile, 11 yds)

Lismore Circus Umbrella Tunnel
2.22 2.17
2.29 4.06
2.06

UP SLOW
DOWN SLOW
UP FAST 2.13
DOWN FAST

2.33

0.03

0.08 0.69

Carlton Rd Jn

1.72

Kentish Town Jn
3.58

0.58
0.65
1.74
1.65

⑧

KENTISH TOWN
3.40 (Moorgate)
1.42 (St Pancras)

[LN 3213]

MCL
LMS : Mid

4.26

• = Planned re-electrification 2007

Camden Rd Jn Dalston Western Jn
(CR) (D)

[LN 101] ECM 1
LNE : GN

14A : to Finsbury Park

[LN 3201] SPC 1
LMS : Mid

Gospel Oak (GO)
Camden Road (CR)

KENTISH TOWN WEST
0.34 ③

W

8C, 5 : 43A
Chiltern Line
(tracks) to Baker St / Marylebone

[MD 701] MCJ LNE : GC CHILTERN LINE

[MD 120] CWJ LNE : LNW

3 : 18D : to Harrow-on-the-Hill

JRN SOUTH HAMPSTEAD
RD 2.33
⑥ ①
① S
② N
DC ELECTRIC

PRIMROSE HILL
5.49 Ω

Sth Hampstead Tunnels
Camden Jn
1.59
[5.75]

UP NL

DOWN BRANCH

Kentish Town Vdct
arches 1 - 94

[EA 1310] BOK 2
LMS : LNW
(NL : Hampstead Jn)

[LN 3201] SPC 1
LMS : Mid

Camden Rd Jn
(CR) 5.09 ⊠ E

arches
35-1 5.23-1.24 25 -101

Camden Rd E. Jn
4.52

3.09
(66 yds)

2.75

Copenhagen Jn 0.00
[0.64]
0.64

Camden Road Tunnels
(205 yds)
1.13
(308 yds)

Dock Jn North 0.76/2.73

0.79

2.59

DOWN N. LONDON No. 1
UP N. LONDON No. 1
UP N. LONDON No. 2
DOWN N. LONDON No. 2

4.20 (0.56)

Barnsbury Jn
3.75

E 2

1B

SPC 1
MCL

Controlled by West Hampstead PSB (WH)

204.37
2.29
2.27
3.02

Primrose Hill Tunnels
(1182 yds)

5.78
1.54
1.51

1.40
1.36
Camden Jn

3

Miles from Euston

[MD 101] LEC 1 LMS : LNW (London & Birmingham)

WEST COAST MAIN LINE

Ω
DN NL
UP NL
5.65

5.57
Primrose Hill Jn

LNW SE
(WM) (CR)

DOWN N. LONDON No. 2 LINES

5.35 5.23
Camden Viaduct
5.42

0.00 5.09
5.10
Camden Rd West Jn

5.23

CAMDEN RD 5.01
(AC/DC changeover)

4.64 (0.51)
Camden Rd 4.57

UP *P N.LON. INCLINE
DN

4.48

4.72 UP N.L.

W
Camden Rd
Central Jn

M

4 : 1 : to London Euston

2 CRC 1
LMS : NL
[MD 145] (Hampstead Rd Jn)

From Camden Road West Jn ALL directions are DOWN & Line Designations change

[EA 1320] BOK 1

4 : 1 : to London St Pancras

4 : 1 : to Farringdon, Blackfriars & Moorgate

5
Miles from former Broad Street Station

* P N. LON. INCLINE

0.20

★ CTRL

0.55

0.46

14A : to Kings Cross

CALEDONIAN ROAD AND BARNSBURY
3.74 ⑥ Ω

W 1

BOK 1
[EA 1320]

Ω = Primrose Hill to Caledonian Road & Barnsbury
North London Line Viaducts and Arches

Locations	Arches
5.35-5.23	35 - 1
5.23-5.09	1 - 24
5.09-5.01	25 -47
5.01-4.66	48 - 94
4.53-4.51	98 - 100
4.23-4.17	108 - 116

M = Maintenance Sdg
SE LNE
(CR) (K)

2 CRF 1
NLI
[EA 1320][LN 115]

CTRL 5 : 49A
to CTRL

★ = 0.55 Belle Isle points connections distorted to clarify layouts
★ = 0.44 Future Camden Rd Incline Jn
✳ = 0.13 Future York Way North Jn

EUSTON to WATFORD ELECTRIC & NORTH LONDON LINES
Platforms are designated by poster bills and / or platform nos. as :
'Northbound' i.e. to Watford or 'Southbound' i.e. Euston
'Eastbound' i.e. to N. Woolwich or 'Westbound' i.e. Richmond

B

14B : to Alexandra Palace

[EA 1370][LN 115]
SE LNE
(HP) (K)
LNE HPW

Harringay Jn
3.29
0.03

HARRINGAY
3.32

SEVEN SISTERS
5.48

5.52

10B : to Enfield Town & Cheshunt

10B : to Cheshunt

[EA 1160] BGK LNE : GE

TOTTENHAM HALE
6.00 ⑫

arches
6.13 6.22

6.56-62
6.35

Lea Valley Viaduct

BLACKHORSE ROAD
7.21 ④

10B : to Chingford

UPPER HOLLOWAY
3.00 ⑥

[EA 1370] TAH 1
LNE & LMS Jt
(Tottenham & Hampstead Jt)

Harringay Park Jn
(HP) 4.12

0.14
DN
0.25
4.15

Hornsey Train Servicing Centre

HARRINGAY GREEN LANES
4.61 ⑪

3.20 4.29

5.56

5.30

Seven Sisters Jn
5.40/0.00

SSL [EA 1300]
LNE:GE

0.13

5.65
S. Tott. West Jn

5.73 S. Tott. East Jn

UP TOTT. CVE
DOWN TOTT. CVE

5.55

Tottenham South Jn
5.41

7

8

5.79
8.05

WALTHAMSTOW QUEENS ROAD
8.11 ⑨

3A

[EA 1370] TAH 2
LMS : Mid
(Tottenham & Forest Gate Jn Rly)

1A

DOWN T & H
UP T & H

Upper Holloway (UH)
2.76

CROUCH HILL
3.65

4.01-4.05
Crown Hill Tunnel
(90 yards)

14B : to King's Cross

[LN 101] ECM 1
LNE : GN

SOUTH TOTTENHAM 5.69
S. Tottenham Jn (S) 5.71

1 TAH 2
[EA 1370]

Coppermill (North) Jn

4.74

Clapton Jn
4.38

Temple Mills & Stratford

SSL = UP & DN SEVEN SISTERS CHORD

10B

[EA 1290]
1 TSE 2
Tottenham West Jn
★COM

S. Tottenham (S) | Liverpool St (L)
6.22 | 5.54

10B

3
Miles from St Pancras

4 5

Miles from St Pancras

14A : to Finsbury Park

Canonbury Tunnel

[LN 110] CFP LNE : GN

Barnsbury Jn
3.75

Canonbury W. Jn E. Jn
3.21
3.20
3.12

LNE (KING'S X (K)) LNE : GN
SE (D) LMS : NL [EA 1320]

DALSTON KINGSLAND
2.06 ③

10B
COM
Navarino Rd Jn

B = 2.72
C = 3.04

Platforms
1 ⑩
2-4 ⑨

HACKNEY DOWNS
2.78 ①

HOMERTON
2.01 ③

HACKNEY WICK
2.68 ⑥

River Lea
3.18

2B to Stratford

UP & DN N.L. No. 1
2.66 2.21
UP N.L. No. 1
DN N.L. No. 1
1.40

DOWN N.L. No. 2
UP NORTH LONDON No. 2

Dalston Western Jn
(D) 2.16

Dalston Jn

Reading Lane Jn 2.55

§

1.11 1.18
2.79 DN CURVE

2.65

3.04

C
B

2.68
3.04

arch 452

165 - 225 arches

Victoria Park

DOWN WOOLWICH
UP WOOLWICH
1.40 1.72 2.40

1.32

2.69

1A

E 2 E 7 2 E 2

W 1 W 1

CALEDONIAN ROAD AND BARNSBURY
3.74 ⑥

HIGHBURY & ISLINGTON
3.36 ⑥

CANONBURY
2.73 ⑥

1 BOK DWW 1
[EA 1320] LMS : NL

(D) (L)
[EA 1180] GRE
BR

HACKNEY CENTRAL ⑥
(D) (S) Liverpool St

1 DWW 2
(Victoria Park Jn)
2.48 (0.00)
LMS : NL LNE : GE

4 3 3
Miles from former Broad St Station
(but reverses at Dalston Western Jn to Navarino Rd Jn)

Miles from Liverpool Street 2 —

LONDON FIELDS
2.35 ⑩

DOWN SUBURBAN
UP SUBURBAN
DOWN FAST
UP FAST

GRAHAM RD
UP CURVE

arches 319-321 2.35
arch 396

arch 290

1.74 Regent's Canal

arches 319-321
1.61
arch 290

CAMBRIDGE HEATH
1.61

2A : to Liverpool St.

Present day mileage origin for lines to North Woolwich and Navarino Rd Jn

[EA 1160] BGK LNE : GE

Controlled by Liverpool Street IECC (L)

© Copyright TRACKmaps. No reproduction without permission

A

Controlled by Liverpool Street IECC (S)

10B : to Temple Mills

Ø Miles from Channelsea North Jn

Temple Mills East Jn   0.59   4.45
Temple Mills Lane   4.46   4.45
4.10

[EA 1280] SDC   LNE : GE (Northern & Eastern Railway)

Miles from Liverpool street   1   5

[EA 1010] LTN 1   LNE : GE (Eastern Counties)

Stratford International West Jn   10.15km

Stratford International East Jn   5 : 49A

Maryland East Crossovers   4.43

DOWN MAIN   UP MAIN   DOWN ELECTRIC   UP ELECTRIC

4.56   4.62

MARYLAND   4   2   3   1

4.00/4.03   STRATFORD

High Meads Loop
London Tunnel 1   9.08km
Down Int'nl   4   9.72km
3 Dn Domestic   9.30km
2 Up Domestic
1 Up International

CTRL under construction

STRATFORD INTERNATIONAL (from St Pancras)   9.47km
Plms 1 & 4   390m
Plms 2 & 3   270m

Stratford Low Level Tunnel (77 yds)

5 : 37C : London Underground (Central Line)

−4 Miles from former Victoria Park Jn

[EA 1320] DWW 2   LNE : GE (Eastern Counties & Thames Jn Railway)
4.19 (Stratford Market)

STRATFORD LOW LEVEL 3.70

Bridge 612 (High St)   4.06

DOWN WOOLWICH   UP WOOLWICH
WESTBOUND   EASTBOUND

LUL JUBILEE LINE

Stratford Market Depot

STRATFORD Platforms
5 ⑫
8 ⑫
9 ⑫
10 ⑫
10A ⑫
11, 12 ⑧

Controlled by Neasden

London LIVERPOOL STREET   0.00

Platforms
1
2-8
9
10
11
12
13
14-15
16-18

⑫ ⑫ ⑫ ⑭ ⑬ ⑬ ⑬ ⑬ ⑧

1B & 10B : to Hackney Downs

[EA 1160] BGK   LNE : GE
arch 290   1.61

CAMBRIDGE HEATH   1.61

Bethnal Green North Jn   1.30

[EA 1010] LTN 1   LNE : GE (Eastern Counties)

Bethnal Green West Jn (0.62)

BETHNAL GREEN

Bethnal Green East Jn

Liverpool Street IECC (L) also Stratford (North London) (S)

Bishopsgate Tunnel (627 yds)

Wheler St Jn or Bishopsgate Jn (for East London Line)

[EA 1010] LTN 1   LNE : GE

Platform access at Liverpool Street
1-10 with SUBURBAN LINES
5-14 with MAIN LINES
13-18 with ELECTRIC LINES

B

Miles from Liverpool street

Lea Junction   3.19/0.51 $

River Lea   3.18

1B : to Hackney Wick

High Meads Jn 0.65 (miles from 0.00 at former Victoria Park Jn)

[EA 1340] LLS 2   LNE : GE

[EA 1350] CHM   LNE : GE

Channelsea North Jn #[0.29] $(0.65)

Channelsea South Jn #[0.29] $(0.70)   3.33

Carpenters Road North Junction 2.48 (0.00)

[EA 1020] CNS   LNE : GE

Carpenters Road South Jn $ LL.12

[EA 1150] CST   LNE : GE

CHANNELSEA CURVE   0.15   0.00

DOWN WOOLWICH   UP WOOLWICH
DOWN ELECTRIC   UP ELECTRIC
DOWN MAIN   UP MAIN

Stratford Central Jn

Stratford East   3.65

DOCKLANDS LIGHT RAILWAY

Wharton Road Bridge (56)   3.46

Proposed DLR Diversion

Thornton Fields Carriage Sidings (TF)   9, 10, 15 N/RU, 16-33 OOU

East Shunt Spur

Thornton Fields Jn   3.32

Marshgate Sidings

Waste Transfer Station

Bow Midland Waste Recycling (Closed)

Bow Depot

PUDDING MILL LANE

[BDM] LMS : Mid

Bow Depot

Wick Lane : EWS Plasmor

River Lea

Bardon Aggregates

Regents Canal   2.03

[EA 1400] GFB   LNE : GE (London & Blackwell Extn)

5 : 48 to Poplar

5 : 45A : to Barking

3A : to Barking

BOW RD

GAS FACTORY CURVE   arches 503-579

Gas Factory Jn

[EA 1010] LTN 1   LNE : GE (Eastern Counties)

Mile End (Devonshire St) OOU

[EA 1320] DWW 2   LNE : GE EC & T Jn](N. Woolwich Rly)

CANNING TOWN

LUL : JUBILEE LINE

WEST HAM   4.08 (High Level) ⑫   4.70 (Low Level) ⑥

5 : 45A : to Barking

3A : to Fenchurch St

C

Controlled by Liverpool Street IECC (S)

North Woolwich Old Station Museum

NORTH WOOLWICH   8.57 ⑥

8   Miles from former Victoria Park Jn

SILVERTOWN   7.77 ⑥

Silvertown Tunnel (600 yds)

5 : 48 : to Beckton

CUSTOM HOUSE   6.72 ⑧

DOCKLANDS LIGHT RAILWAY

ROYAL VICTORIA   CUSTOM HOUSE for Excel   PRINCE REGENT

5 : 47B : to London Bridge, Waterloo & Stanmore

5 : 48 : to Poplar

3A : to Fenchurch St

3A : to Whitechapel   5 : 45A

DOWN WOOLWICH   UP WOOLWICH
EB DISTRICT   WB DISTRICT
DOWN MAIN   UP MAIN

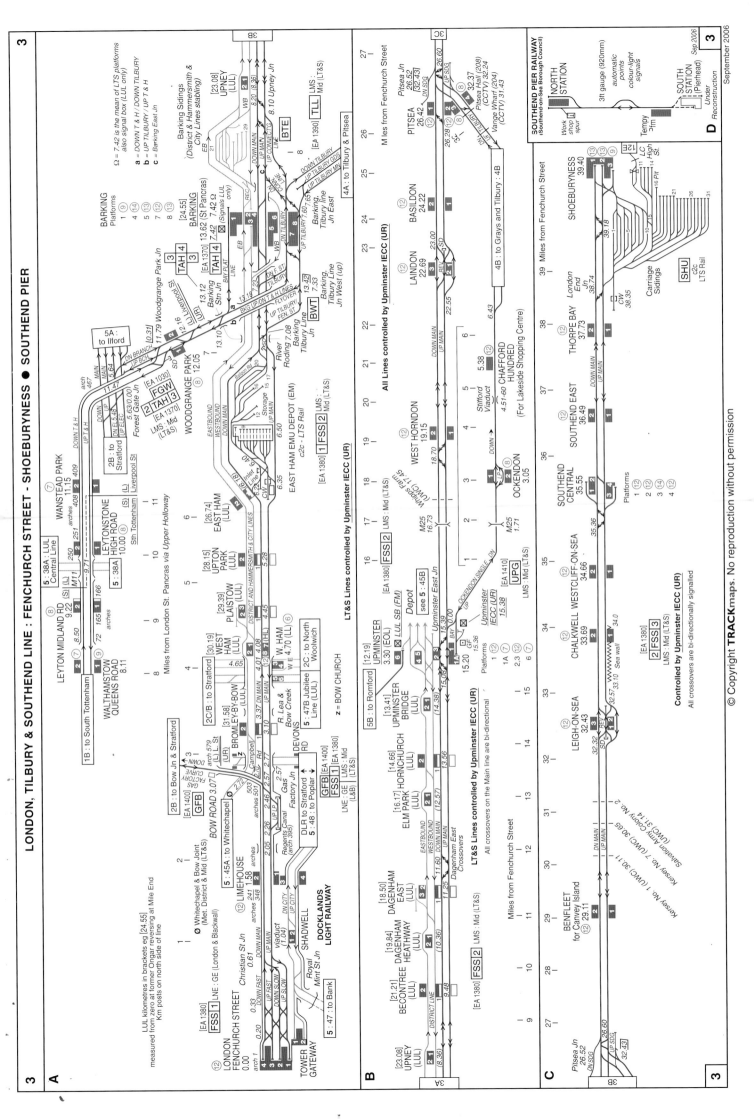

LONDON, TILBURY & SOUTHEND LINE : FENCHURCH STREET - SHOEBURYNESS ● SOUTHEND PIER

September 2006

© Copyright TRACKmaps. No reproduction without permission

LONDON, TILBURY & SOUTHEND LINE : TILBURY LOOP ● AUDLEY END RLY ● COLNE VALLEY RLY ● STANSTED AIRPORT PEOPLEMOVER

A

Miles from Fenchurch Street

RIPPLE LANE RAILHEAD [RLY]
8.60-10.37

Controlled by Upminster IECC (UR)

HOWARD TENENS

DOWN TILBURY MAIN
UP TILBURY MAIN
8.60 UP TILBURY GDS
Ripple Ripple Lane
Lane West Yard
West Jn

Barking,
Tilbury Line Jn East
7.65
7.60
DOWN TILBURY MAIN
UP TILBURY MAIN
Barking Line

3A: Barking

Manor Sdgs (OOU)
17.51

8.40 Ripple Lane East Jn (Up Tilbury/Goods) 9.63
Ripple Lane West Jn (Down Tilbury/Goods) 10.27

9.20
9.31 Renwick Road Jn
9.52 (UR) (ES)
DOWN GOODS
UP GDS
THROUGH SDG
FLT West GSP
9.50
9.54 Stora GSP
Barking/ Ripple Lane
Freightliner Terminal
FLT East GSP
10.06
Temporary Points
Ripple Lane Exchange Sdgs

ACR Logistics
Engrs
10.27 UP TILBURY MAIN
10.45 DAGENHAM DOCK
A13 10.37

East London Waste Terminal-Shanks
Former Car Loading Ramps
Car Loading Ramps
RECEPTION
Down Sdgs
10.67
Ford Gate 5
11.28

* NR 10.60 Close
CTRL 21km
CTRL RAILHEAD
CTRL RP DOWN CHORD
LC No. 2 NECK
No. 1 NECK

Ford Motor Co.
Qy
Hanson Aggregates Terminal
Ramps
CAR STOP LOADING
LC A13 LC

a = Ripple Lane East Jn (Up Tilbury/Goods) 9.63
b = Ripple Lane West Jn (Down Tilbury/Goods) 10.27
c = Chequers Lane (Pedestrian) (103) CCTV 10.49

CTRL Chainage
e = North London Tunnel 2 Portal 20.07 km
f = Dagenham Docks East Jn (Down) 20.83 km
g = Dagenham Docks East Jn (Up) 21.70 km

* = CTRL RP DOWN CHORD
F = FORD'S CONNECTING LINE
H = HANSON CONNECTING LINE

d = CONNECTING LINE

Manor Way (112) CCTV 12.12
Rainham Creek (River Ingrebourne)
RAINHAM 12.54
12.42

(114) CCTV 12.60

Esso 16.38
Thames Board Mills (MCB) 16.38
Deep Wharf 16.65
Manor Way (137) 16.49
Jurgens (138) (MCB) 17.09
Q.E. Bridge
Purfleet Jn S 17.45
17.55
17.61
CTRL Thurrock Vdct 17.39

Foster Yeoman
Purfleet Deep Wharf
Purfleet Thames Terminal

[EA 1390] CTRL Aveley Viaduct 14.60/14.70
A13 14.20
[5 - 49C]
Purfleet Rifle Range (129) (UWG) 15.27

PURFLEET 16.02/16.12
Purfleet Long Sdg Jn N
(132) (CCTV) 16.07

[TLL] LMS: Mid (LT & S)

DOWN TILBURY
UP TILBURY
LONG SDGS
Manor (Thames Matex/Vopark)
former Van den Burghs & Jurgens (OOU)

w = Jurgens Long Sdg
x = Vellacots Long Sdg
z = Inter-modal Terminal

B

Miles from Upminster

Miles from Fenchurch Street

[EA 1410] [UPG]
3B: to Upminster

Vellacots (146) (UWG) 17.61
18.38
18.65
West Thurrock Jn 19.03
[6.56]
THIRD LINE 19.52
[6.43]
DN TILBURY
UP TILBURY

West Thurrock Sdgs (OOU)

High Street (SS) (CCTV) 19.76
Grays East Jn 20.01
GRAYS 19.70
Seabrook Sdgs

Platforms
1   8
2   9
3   5

Controlled by Upminster IECC (UR)

Walton Common (184) (UWG) 23.40
Manor Way (189) 24.02
Low Street (CCTV) 24.11
Coal Road 24.43

TILBURY TOWN 21.48
Tilbury Town Jn
Tilbury Railport Jn 22.30
Tilbury East Jn (former Tilbury West Jn) 22.06

DN TILBURY
UP TILBURY
Tilbury RCT: Freightliners
CRANE ROAD A
CRANE ROAD B

TILBURY
Exchange Sdgs
Northfleet Hope Terminal
Tilbury Dock
Tilbury Container Services
Container Stacking Area
LC
RR
Tilbury Grain Terminal EWS
[TDE]

TILBURY INTERNATIONAL RAIL FREIGHT TERMINAL
PORT (Forth Ports)
Victa Railfreight EWS
Tilbury Riverside Sdgs
Loco Release
CR
ACC/DEP
Loading/Discharge Area

[EA 1390] [TLL]
EAST TILBURY 25.07
Mucking (182) (AHBC) 26.40
Sewage Farm (UWG) 26.75
26.77
UP / DN
26.41 Thames Haven Jn
[EA 1390] LMS: Mid (LT & S)
25.76 (CCTV) 25.07

STANFORD-LE-HOPE 27.13
(225) (CCTV) 27.17
DOWN TILBURY
UP TILBURY
27
28   29

Hydrocracker (235) (AOCL) 29.04
[EA 1420] [THN]
No. 43 Gate (open) 29.18 / 29.8 (236)
LMS: Mid (LT & S) (Thames Haven Dock & Railway)
UP & DOWN THAMES HAVEN
THAMES HAVEN
UP DN
0.00
30.13
30.18
30.40
Coryton BP Oil Refinery
Qy
Shunters' Cabin

Fobbing (189) (AHBCX) 30.36
Gardners (201) (CCTV) 30.75
Vange Wharf (204) (CCTV) 31.11
Mennings (202) (UWG) 30.75
Pitsea Hall (208) (CCTV) 32.24
PITSEA 32.37
32.43
Pitsea Jn 26.52
3C: to Shoeburyness
3B: to Barking

C

AUDLEY END RAILWAY

1⅛" = 96 chains

Gamage's Summit
Whitehouse Curve
Horseshoe Curve
FOREST DEEP HALT
0.42   0.43
0.62
0.23/62
0.19
River Cam
River Fulfen
0.05
0.69
0.82
Water Tower
0.01
0.92
AUDLEY END
Loco PW

Sep 2005

D

COLNE VALLEY RAILWAY CO. LTD.
Colne Valley Railway Preservation Society Ltd.

Former BR mileages shown based on ZERO at Liverpool St via Marks Tey Jn

NB: Former Sible & Castle Hedingham Station at 55M 56ch

CASTLE HEDINGHAM 60.61
Diesel Sdgs
Delivery Sdg GF
Newmans Sdgs
R. Colne
footpath LC
Steam Shed
Delivery Sdg
LOOP
MAIN
60.55
60.43
footpath LC 60.43
60.20
Hedingham North GF 60.55
Nunnery Jn (formerly at Wrabness) 60.43
Nunnery Jn GF

a = Drawell GF
b = Hedingham North GF (formerly at Cressing)
c = Diesel Sidings GF

Length: 63 chains

61.03

Aug 2005

E

STANSTED AIRPORT PEOPLEMOVER

INTERNATIONAL TERMINAL BUILDING
Departures   Arrivals
INTERNATIONAL ARRIVALS
INTERNATIONAL DEPARTURES Gates 11-20
Maintenance Shed

September 2006

© Copyright TRACKmaps. No reproduction without permission

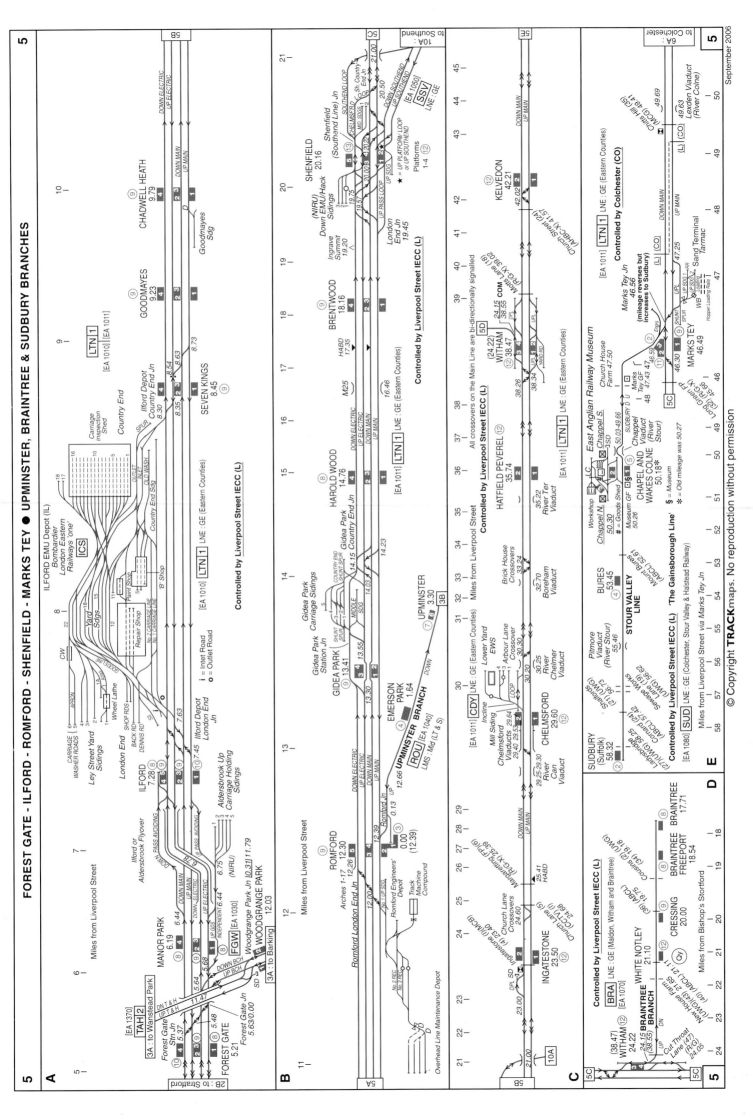

FOREST GATE - ILFORD - ROMFORD - SHENFIELD - MARKS TEY ● UPMINSTER, BRAINTREE & SUDBURY BRANCHES

September 2006

© Copyright TRACKmaps. No reproduction without permission

COLCHESTER - IPSWICH - (NORWICH) ● COLCHESTER - WALTON & CLACTON

A

Controlled by Colchester (CO)

Track Machine Shed

CER LNE : GE

Colchester South Jn

SE : to Marks Tey

Halifax Junction 67.67

Ipswich or Stoke Tunnel (361 yards)
68.47 68.31

DOWN UP

Pluck's Farm (30) (UWG) 62.44
Bentley (53) (AHBC-X) 63.07

River Stour Viaduct 59.71-59.75
Cattawade Viaduct 60.06-60.10

MANNINGTREE 59.35
Manningtree North Jn 00.00
Manningtree South Jn 59.46
Manningtree East Jn 59.74
NTE LNE : GE
9B : to Harwich
[EA 1120]

UP HARWICH
DOWN HARWICH
NORTH CURVE

Ardleigh GSP 56.00
Ardleigh (44) (CCTV) 56.04

DOWN MAIN
UP MAIN

Platforms
1 ⑫ 4 ⑮
2 ⑬ 5 ⑪
3 ⑭ ⑪

Colchester (CO)
(controls to Norwich incl.) Colchester Jn
51.65
51.49 51.52
COLCHESTER (NORTH) 51.52
Colchester Jn 51.37
D & UP SDG
UP PASSENGER LOOP
51.00
51.30
SUDBURY SDG
Locos
LTN 1 [EA 1011]
DOWN MIN UP MAIN

B

Controlled by Thorpe-le-Soken (T)

FRINTON 68.66
WALTON-ON-THE-NAZE 70.15
(Tendring Hundred Extension)
TWN LNE : GE [EA 1110]
Pork Lane (1)(AHBC) Nursery (3) (UWG) 67.32
KIRBY CROSS 67.55
Nursery (5) 66.65

CLACTON 69.56
Emu Sdgs
Down Sdgs
Maint. Depot
3 Maint. Depot
5 Maint. Depot
OUTSIDE RD
MIDDLE RD
KLONDYKE SDG
UP CLACTON 69.42
DOWN CLACTON 69.22
CW RD
DEAD END RD
CW 69.19
CONNECTING LINE
COC LNE : GE (Clacton-on-Sea Railway)
[EA 1090]

THORPE-LE-SOKEN 65.07
Thorpe-le-Soken Jn 65.19
DOWN SDG
Engrs ⑫
65.06 (T)
64.70
Giles (49) (UWG) 67.45
Burrs Road (51) (MCG) 68.04
Three Gates (45) (UWG) 65.59
SINGLE
WALTON

WEELEY 62.78
GREAT BENTLEY 60.66
Thorrington (TH) 59.42
DOWN CLACTON
UP CLACTON

Frating (TH) 59.74
(MCB) 60.02
(MCG) 59.41 (AHBC)
Colchester Road (15) (MCG) 58.07
ALRESFORD (Essex) 57.63
57.52 (MCG) 57.68
(1-t) (MCG) 57.63

WIVENHOE 56.00
HYTHE 53.49
Hythe (8) (UWG) 54.61
Wivenhoe Park (4) (CCTV) 53.54
(Tendring Hundred)   (Tendring Hundred Extension)
COC LNE : GE [EA 1090]

Colne Jn Hythe Jn
East Gate Jn
(MCB) 53.12
53.14 A 53.34
53.36
Hythe 53.36
CTH LNE : GE [EA 1100] (Tendring Hundred)
East Gate Jn (EG) 53.13
STB [EA 1100]
COLCHESTER TOWN 53.76 (formerly ST. BOTOLPHS)
COC LNE : GE [EA 1090]
52.65
52.42
52.35
52.33
52.00
AVOIDING
UP CLAC
DOWN CLACTN
CLACTON SINGLE
Colchester, Stour Valley, Sudbury & Halstead
UP CLACTON SDG

GRW [EA 1130]
Griffin Wharf 0.77 West Bank Terminal
Waterside
Bretts Sdg 6A
RIVER ORWELL
Cliff Quay
Swing Bridge
NEW CUT
Associated British Ports
Ipswich West Bank
Ipswich Lower Yard
Stoke Bridge (AOCL) 1.23
Ranelagh Rd (MCG) 0.56
River Orwell
(NIRU)
IPD [EA 1140]
6C : below

GRW [EA 1130]
To Griffin Wharf
DOWN → 6B
0.00
LNE : GE (Eastern Union Railway)
LTN 1 [EA 1011]
Eastern Counties
LNE : GE [EA 1011]

C

Controlled by Colchester (CO)

STOWMARKET 80.46
ICI Paints
Regent Street (82) (CCTV) 80.68
Marsh Lane (UWC) 80.79
(MCG) 80.54
80.40
U & DGL
DRS
Haughley Jn 82.79/40.49
82.18 (UWC)
CCH LNE : GE [EA 1530]
12D : to Bury St Edmunds
Haughley Jn 82.79/40.49 40.46

GSP 85.20
Cow Green Emergency Crossover
Gislingham 88.14 (UWC)
(Finningham) 86.45
Wissick (90) (AHBC) 82.70
Newton Flotman (31) (AHBC-X) 108.19
Swainsthorpe (33) (AHBC-X) 109.54

NEEDHAM MARKET 77.07
Badley Viaduct 79.08 (River Gipping)
Gypsy Lane (76) 77.64 (UWC)
Barham
Tilbury Roadstone / Lafarge Aggregates
74.12
Bawham (AHBC-X) 75.17
DGL
DN MAIN
UP MAIN
Claydon (88) (CCTV) 73.47
Daines Mayhew (69) (UWC) 72.75
(Qv)

East Suffolk Jn 69.57
69.41
DOWN MAIN 69.27
DN & UP STDFT
UP MAIN 69.27
ESK LNE : GE [EA 1430]
9A : to Felixstowe & Woodbridge
London Road
IUP London Road
Upper Yd: EWS
(NIRU)

Ipswich Goods Jn 68.72
68.75
IPSWICH 68.59
Loco Fuelling Point
Ranelagh Rd (MCG) 0.56
68.47
Ipswich Platforms
4a 4b 4c ⑫
3a 3b ⑫
2 ⑫
1a 1b ⑫
LONDON END
SN 1 SN 2
I. FIELD
Carriage Sidings
IPD [EA 1140]
6A
6B : above
[EA 1011] [EA 1012]
LTN 1 LNE : GE (Ipswich & Bury St Edmunds Railway)
[EA 1012]
River Orwell

DISS 94.79
Palgrave (120) (AHBC-X) 94.04
94.65 94.54
River Waveney Viaduct
UP THRO SDG
LTN 1 LNE : GE (Ipswich & Bury St Edmunds Railway) [EA 1012]
95.22
Mellis (116) (AHBC-X) 91.34
Rectory Road (119) (AHBC-X) 91.16

D

7A : to Norwich

ETN [EA 1580]
Lakenham Viaduct (inc. River Yare)
121.57
Tharston Viaduct (River Tas) 105.62
Flordon Emergency Crossover 106.63
Tivetshall (9) (AHBC-X) 100.43
Black Mill (10) 101.01
Mounton (16) (AHBC-X) 101.51
Hales Street (AHBC-X) 100.26
Burston (128) (AHBC-X) 97.47
Audley End (Norfolk) (126) (AHBC-X) 97.04
Gissing (No. 2) (AHBC-X) 98.57
Beacon (Wright) (114) (UWC) 91.16
13B : to Wymondham
112.25 112.32 112.33
121.57

DOWN MAIN
UP MAIN

6C 6D

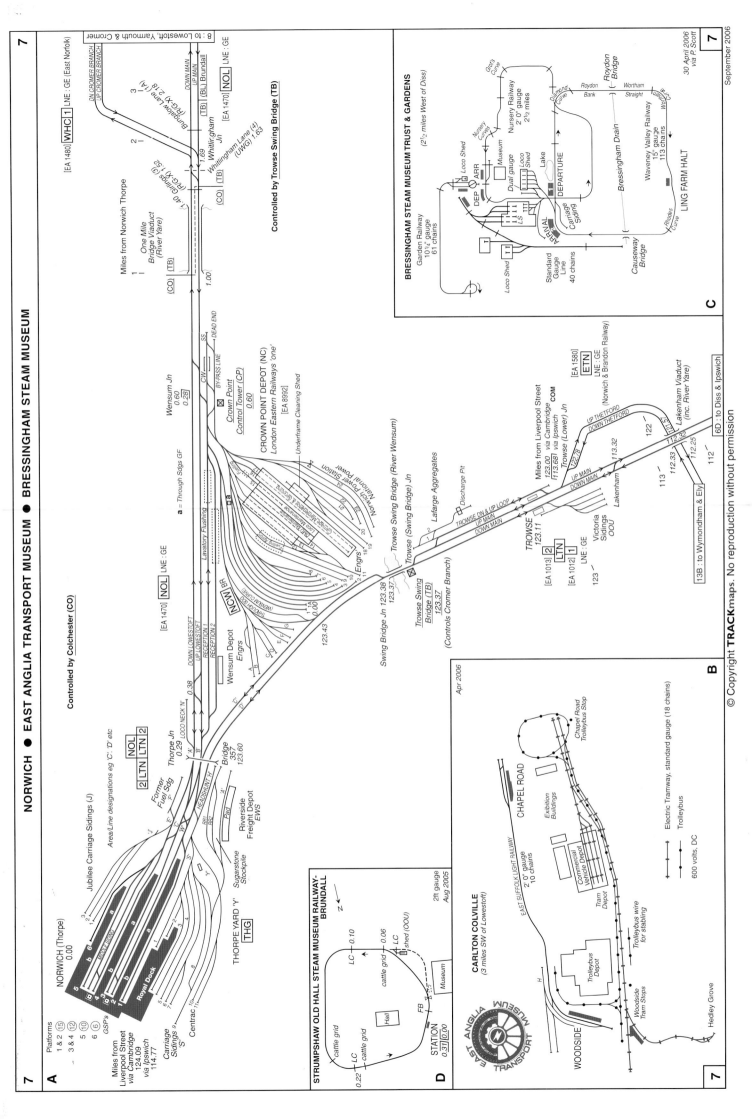

NORWICH ● EAST ANGLIA TRANSPORT MUSEUM ● BRESSINGHAM STEAM MUSEUM

A — Controlled by Colchester (CO)

NORWICH (Thorpe) 0.00

Miles from Liverpool Street via Cambridge 124.09 via Ipswich 114.77

Platforms
1 & 2 (15)
3 & 4 (12)
5 (10)
6 (6)

Jubilee Carriage Sidings (J)

Area/Line designations eg 'C' 'D' etc

2 LTN NOL LNE : GE
2 LTN NOL

Former Fuel Stg
Thorpe Jn
LOCO NECK 'N'
0.29

Carriage Sidings 'S'
Centrac
Sugarstone Stockpile

THORPE YARD 'Y'
THG

Bridge 357 123.60

Riverside Freight Depot EWS

Wensum Depot
Engrs
NCW BR

RECEPTION 1
RECEPTION 2
DOWN LOWESTOFT
UP LOWESTOFT
0.38

a = Through Sdgs GF

Lavatory Flushing

Norwich National Power

CROWN POINT DEPOT (NC)
London Eastern Railways 'one'
[EA 8992]

Undertrame Cleaning Shed

Crown Point Control Tower (CP) 0.60

Wensum Jn 0.60 0.28

BY-PASS LINE
DEAD END
CW SS

123.43

Trowse Swing Bridge (River Wensum)

Swing Bridge Jn 123.38 123.37

Trowse (Swing Bridge) Jn

Trowse Swing Bridge (TB) 123.37
(Controls Cromer Branch)

Lafarge Aggregates
Discharge Pit

TROWSE 123.11
2 LTN
[EA 1013] [EA 1012] LNE : GE
123

Victoria Sidings OOU
Lakenham

Miles from Liverpool Street 123.00 via Cambridge 113.681 via Ipswich COM

UP THETFORD
DOWN THETFORD
Trowse (Lower) Jn
UP MAIN
DOWN MAIN
TROWSE DN & UP LOOP

122.78
113.32
122
113
112.33
112.32
112.25
112.54
112

[EA 1580] ETN LNE : GE (Norwich & Brandon Railway)

Lakenham Viaduct (inc. River Yare)

6D : to Diss & Ipswich
13B : to Wymondham & Ely

Miles from Norwich Thorpe
One Mile Bridge Viaduct (River Yare)
1.00

Whitlingham (UWG) 1.63
Whitlingham Jn 1.69

DN CROMER BRANCH
UP CROMER BRANCH

[EA 1480] WHC 1 LNE : GE (East Norfolk)

3 (1A) 2.18
Bungalow Lane (R.C. × 1)
Gillings (R.C. × 1) 1.52
Whitlingham (R.G. × 1) (3)

DOWN MAIN
UP MAIN
(BL) Brundall
[EA 1470] NOL LNE : GE

8 : to Lowestoft, Yarmouth & Cromer

Controlled by Trowse Swing Bridge (TB)

[EA 1470] NOL LNE : GE

B

BRESSINGHAM STEAM MUSEUM TRUST & GARDENS
(2½ miles West of Diss)

Garden Railway 10¼" gauge 61 chains
Loco Shed
Museum
Dual gauge
Loco Shed
Lake
Gro's Curve
Nursery Railway 2' 0" gauge 2½ miles
Nursery Curves

DEP ARR
ARRIVAL DEPARTURE
LS
T T
Carriage Siding

Standard Gauge Line 40 chains
Loco Shed

Diamond Curve
Roydon Bank
Roydon Bridge
Wortham Straight

Waveney Valley Railway 15" gauge 113 chains

Bressingham Drain
Causeway Bridge
Phebs Curve

LING FARM HALT

30 April 2006 via P. Scott

C

STRUMPSHAW OLD HALL STEAM MUSEUM RAILWAY - BRUNDALL

2ft gauge
Aug 2005

cattle grid
LC 0.10
LC 0.06
cattle grid
shed (OOU)
Hall
STATION 0.00
0.31
Museum
FB
cattle grid
LC
0.22
cattle grid

D

EAST ANGLIA TRANSPORT MUSEUM

CARLTON COLVILLE
(3 miles SW of Lowestoft)

Apr 2006

CHAPEL ROAD
Chapel Road Trolleybus Stop

EAST SUFFOLK LIGHT RAILWAY 2' 0" gauge 10 chains

Exibition Buildings
Commercial Vehicle Depot
Tram Depot

WOODSIDE
Trolleybus Depot

Woodside Tram Stops
Trolleybus wire for stabling

Hedley Grove

Electric Tramway, standard gauge (18 chains)
Trolleybus
600 volts, DC

September 2006

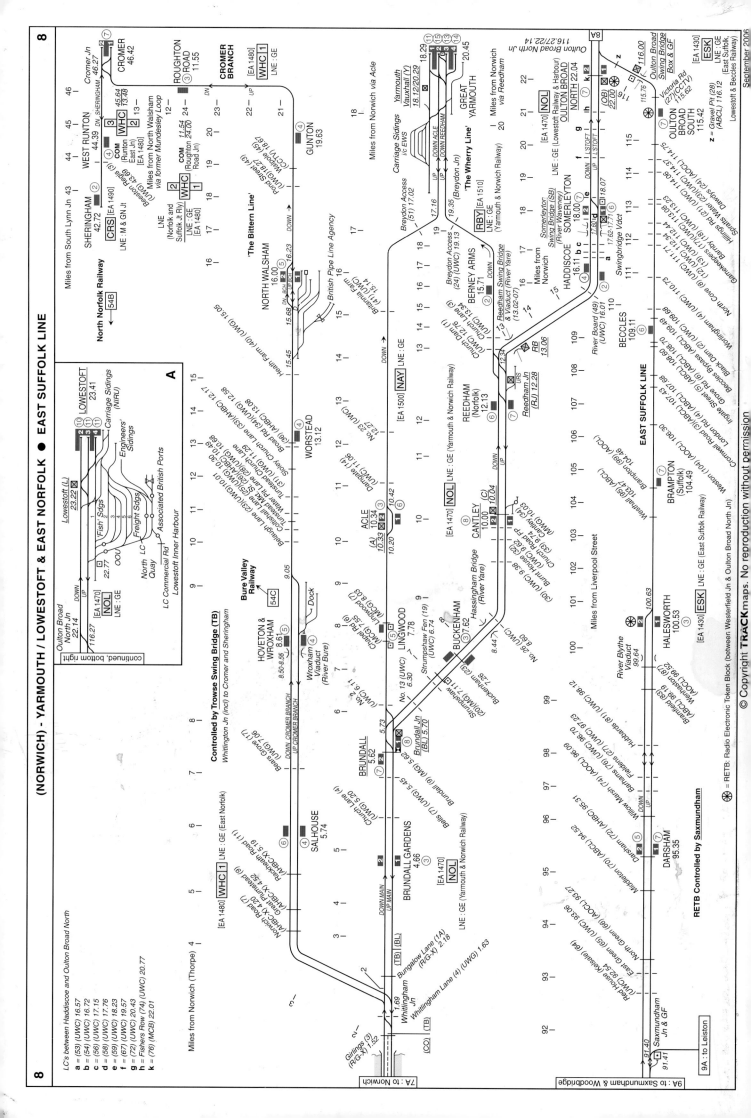

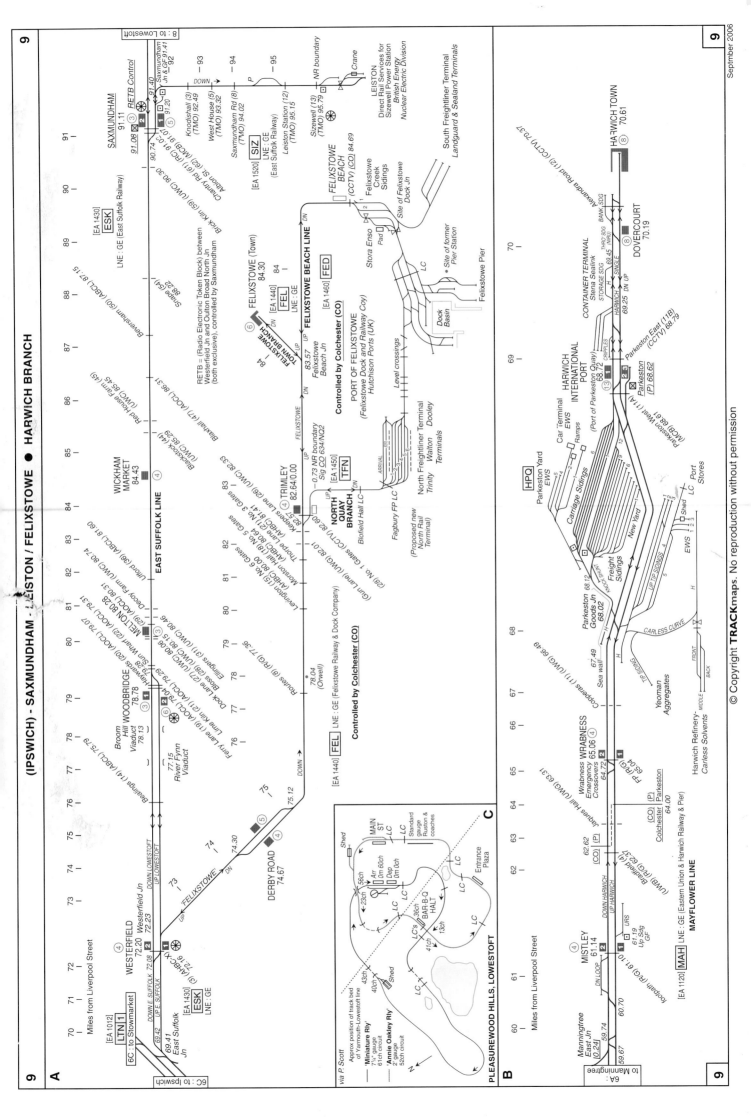

(IPSWICH) - SAXMUNDHAM - LEISTON / FELIXSTOWE ● HARWICH BRANCH

Septmber 2006

SHENFIELD & SOUTHMINSTER BRANCH ● NORTH-EAST LONDON SUBURBAN LINES

A

B

British Energy Nuclear Electric Division

45.30 GF ⓖ — DRS Engrs

Crane ⓖ

Goldens (10) 44.33 (UWC)

SOUTHMINSTER 45.42

Royal Mail Terminal (OOU)

Down Carriage Sdgs (South)

SOUTHEND VICTORIA 41.42

Creasey Piece No. 1 (UWC) 41.18

Stokes Hall (31) (UWC) 40.63

Clifford Farm (30) (UWC) 40.31

Great Sandfords (26) (UWC) 39.27

BURNHAM-ON-CROUCH 43.24

CW

41.41

41.11

Up Carriage Sidings (South)

Up Carriage Sidings (North) (LER)

Down Carriage Sdgs (North) (LER)

ALTHORNE 40.27

PRITTLEWELL 40.67

ROCHFORD 38.54

'CROUCH VALLEY LINE'

FAMBRIDGE 37.23

Rookery No. 1 (19) (UWC) 36.07

Little Hayes (14) (UWC) 36.55

Hogwell (17) (UWC) 34.77

Sommines (13) 34.66 (ABC)

Woodham Ferrers 33.58 (UWC) 33.56

Tabrums Cross (2) (UWC) 33.39

HOCKLEY 36.10

WOODHAM FERRERS 34.00

RAYLEIGH 33.09

[EA 1050] SSV LNE : GE

[EA 1060] WIS LNE : GE

BATTLESBRIDGE 31.40

Controlled by Liverpool Street (L)

All crossovers on the Southend Lines are bi-directionally signalled

DOWN SOUTHEND / UP SOUTHEND

'SOUTHMINSTER'

WICKFORD 29.02

Platforms 1 & 4 ... 5, 12 ... 2 & 3, 12

DRS / URS

Stoke Newington Tunnel (60 yards)

BILLERICAY 24.28

[EA 1050] SSV LNE : GE

Mountnessing Jn 21.32

5C : to Chelmsford

SOUTHEND LOOP

CHELMSFORD LOOP

Shenfield Jn 20.22

SHENFIELD 20.16

5B : to Romford

a = UP PASSENGER LOOP or UP SOUTHEND
b = UP PLATFORM LOOP or UP SOUTHEND

11A : to Cheshunt

Park Lane (MCG) 13.15

Trinity Lane (MCG) 13.22

ENFIELD TOWN 10.55

Platform GF (L)

THEOBALDS GROVE 13.45

13.51 arches

WALTHAM CROSS 12.63

ENT (Enfield & Edmonton)

[EA 1170] LNE : GE

TURKEY STREET 12.16

12.69

13.43

M25 12.35

M25

ENFIELD LOCK 11.65

(15) (CCTV) (L) 11.70

DOWN SOUTHBURY / UP SOUTHBURY

[EA 1190] HDT

Lincoln Road (MCG) 10.25

BUSH HILL PARK 9.69

9.20

[EA 1160] BGK LNE : GE (Northern & Eastern Railway)

BRIMSDOWN 10.61

SOUTHBURY 10.32

Controlled by Liverpool Street IECC (L)

CHINGFORD 10.33

Stn GF

Country End Sidings (Bottom Yard)

London End Sidings (Top Yard)

Carriage Sidings

WASHER RD

CW

10.07

Platforms 1 / 2 & 3

EDMONTON GREEN 8.45

Bury 9.20

White Hart Lane GF 7.36

(CCTV) (L) 10.72

(13) (CCTV) (L) 10.65

PONDERS END 9.71

WHITE HART LANE 7.11

SILVER STREET 7.75

6.73-7.03 arches

513-535 / 6.28

South Tottenham West Jn 5.65 [0.13]

[EA 1300] SSL LNE : GE

ANGEL ROAD 7.57

NORTHUMBERLAND PARK 6.73

[EA 1200] CJC LNE : GE

Controlled by Liverpool Street IECC (L)

HIGHAMS PARK 8.52

(CCTV) 8.45

WOOD STREET 7.07

Hoe Street Tunnel (71 yards)

SEVEN SISTERS 5.48

Seven Sisters GF

4.61 miles from St. Pancras

513-535

DN 7.00.00

South & DN SEVEN SISTERS CHORD / SEVEN SISTERS CHORD

[EA 1370] TAH 1

TAH 2 [EA 1370]

5.52 / 5.40

5.30

TOTTENHAM HALE

LUL Victoria Line Depot

5 : 40C

LMS : Mid (Tottenham & Forest Gate Jn Railway)

BLACKHORSE ROAD 7.21

WALTHAMSTOW CENTRAL 6.16

6.49-52

6.12

LEYTON MIDLAND ROAD 9.22

8.50 8.52 72 arches 165 arches

Miles from St. Pancras

3A : to WoodGrange Park

HARRINGAY GREEN LANES 4.61

STAMFORD HILL 5.03

6.22 / 5.54

Coppermill (North) Jn 4.74

[EA 1290] TSE

South Tottenham Stn 5.71

SOUTH TOTTENHAM 5.69

South Tottenham East Jn 5.73

DOWN T&H / UP T&H

DN T&H / UP T&H

5.56 UP H&T

5.65

6.35

Tottenham South Jn

5.41

Lea Valley Viaduct 6.56-6.62

Tottenham GF

CLAPTON CURVE

ST JAMES STREET 5.55

WALTHAMSTOW QUEENS RD 8.11

Miles from Liverpool Street

1B : to Gospel Oak

*COM 5.54 (L)
(Tottenham West Jn)

6.22 (S)

5.79

50.5

(7)

250

166 arches

[EA 1200] CJC LNE : GE

STOKE NEWINGTON 4.16

4.19-4.22

LEA BRIDGE 4.38

Lea Bridge Rd Vdct

FB

4.29.35 Clapton arches 537-544 (inc. R. Lea)

Clapton Jn 4.38

Controlled by Liverpool Street IECC (S)

Stratford Work Station

RECTORY ROAD 3.64

3.43

[EA 1170] HDT LNE : GE

Clapton Tunnel (284 yards)

Hackney Downs or Queens Road Tunnel (445 yards)

453 arches 512

CLAPTON 3.78

3.66 / 3.53

3.39

Temple Mills West Jn

DOWN TEMPLE MILLS / TEMPLE MILLS

Stratford TMD EWS

Temple Mills Depot Eurostar

Temple Mills Depot Control Room

SDC LNE : GE (Northern & Eastern)

[EA 1280]

(3.21)

(3.15) (3.35) (3.36)

DC / d

CAMBRIDGE HEATH 1.61

LONDON FIELDS 2.35

Miles from Liverpool Street via Stratford

Change of Line Descriptions also
Change of Reverse Mileages

Navarino Road Jn 3.04

1.52 / 1.111

Hackney Downs S. Jn 2.70

HACKNEY DOWNS 2.78

452

Platforms 1 (10), 2-4 (9), 1 (10)

B = 2.72, C = 3.04

a = Washer (Rd)
b = Wheel Condition Mon. Eqpt.
c = Bogie Drop
d = Wheel Lathe

Ruckholt Rd Bridge 5.10

Ruckholt Rd Jn 5.17

5.07

Probable Olympic Sdgs

1B : to Stratford

DWW 1 [EA 1320]

BOGIE DROP RD
WHEEL LATHE RD
FUEL PT RD

(2.60)

(2.28)

2 [EA 1160] GRE BR (LL)

CAMBRIDGE 2.35 (10)

Dalston Jn 1.40

1B : N. London Line to Camden Rd

2.79 / GRAHAM RD CURVE

UP SUBURBAN / DOWN SUBURBAN / DOWN FAST / UP FAST

1.61 / 1.18

290 319-321 396 arch arches

1.61 arch arches

Regent's Canal

[EA 1160] BGK LNE : GE

Controlled by Liverpool Street IECC (L)

§ = Reading Lane Jn 2.55

2.68 / 2.65

Eastway A12 4.65

CTRL Chainage (km) from Stratford International (9.45)/0.00

Temple Mills East Jn 0.59

Temple Mills Lane 4.45 / 4.46

(1.37)

(1.66) Wide to (1.75) gauge

(1.53)

Service LOA RD1 / LOA RD2

4 RECEPTION RDS

(1.46)

Trap points

Temple Mills Depot and Link Line

CTRL Area enclosed by Security Fences

Probable Olympic Sdgs

To Stratford : 2B : to Stratford : 2B : to High Meads Jn.

To Stratford International

2A : to Liverpool Street

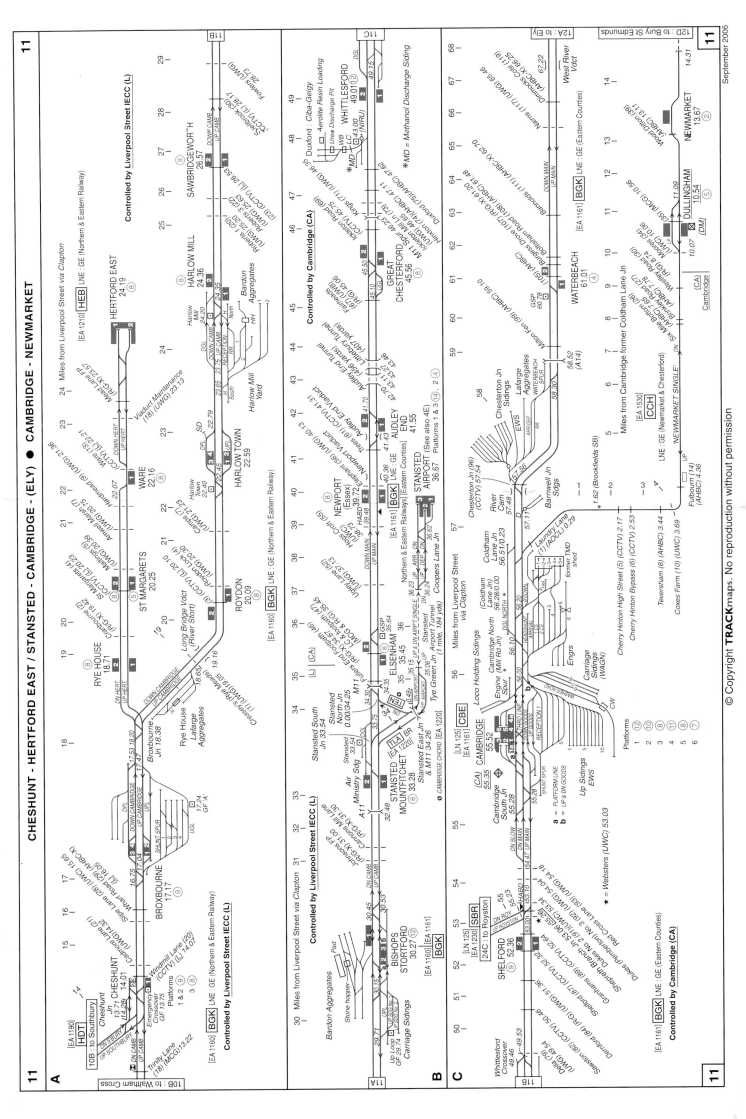

CHESHUNT - HERTFORD EAST / STANSTED - CAMBRIDGE - (ELY) ● CAMBRIDGE - NEWMARKET

September 2006

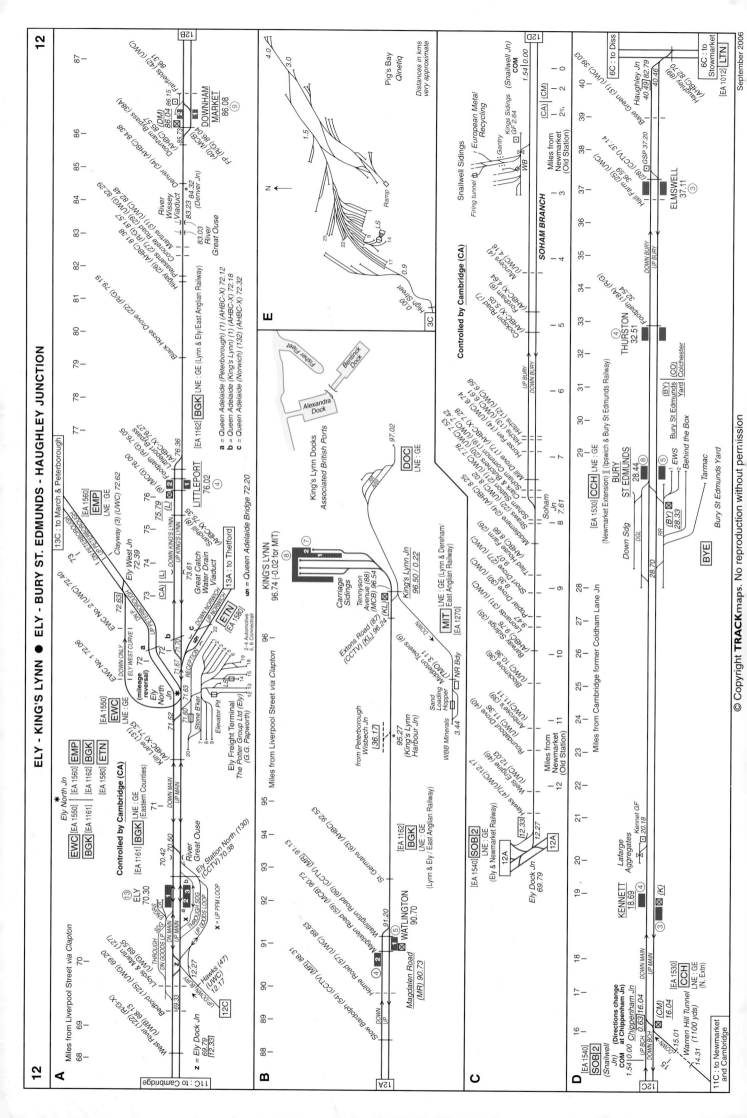

ELY - KING'S LYNN ● ELY - BURY ST. EDMUNDS - HAUGHLEY JUNCTION

September 2006

BRECKLAND LINE : ELY - (NORWICH) ● NORTH ELMHAM BRANCH ● (PETERBOROUGH) - MARCH - (ELY)

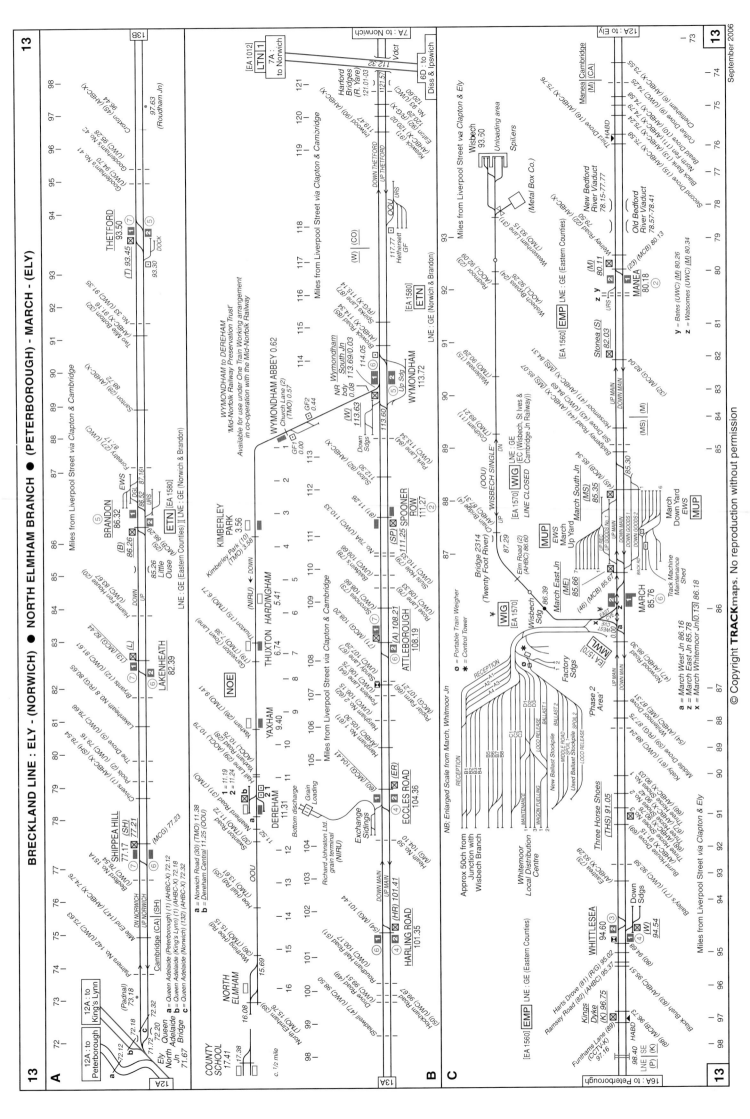

September 2006

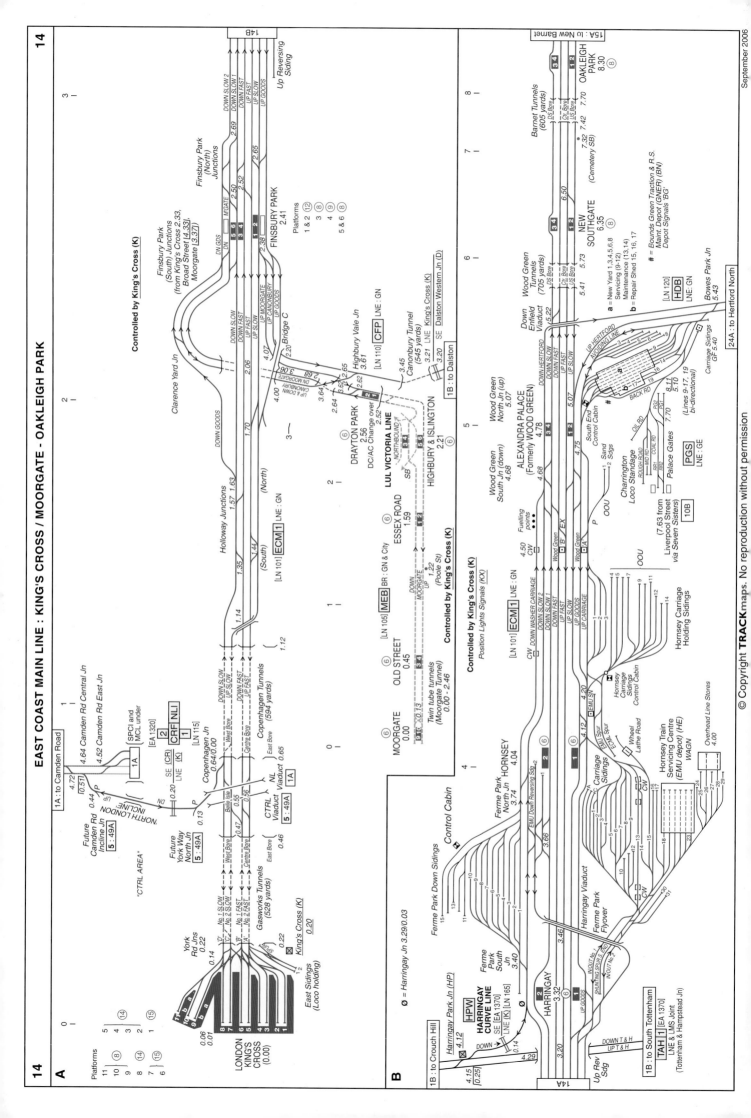

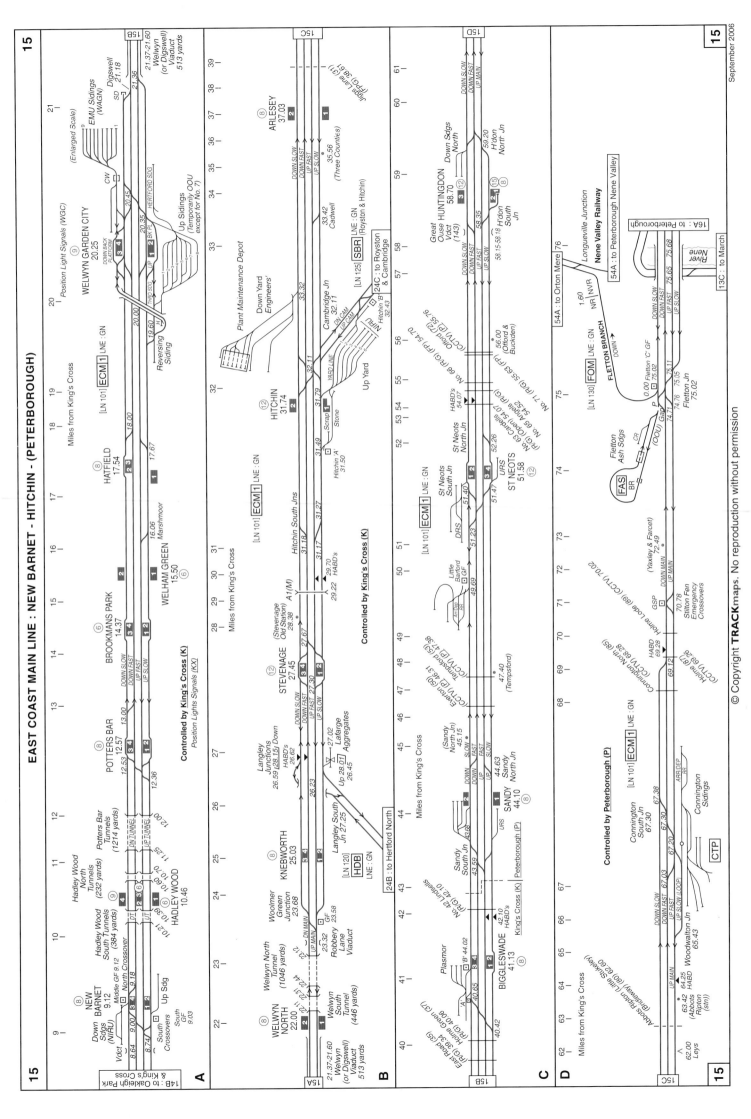

EAST COAST MAIN LINE : NEW BARNET - HITCHIN - (PETERBOROUGH)

September 2006

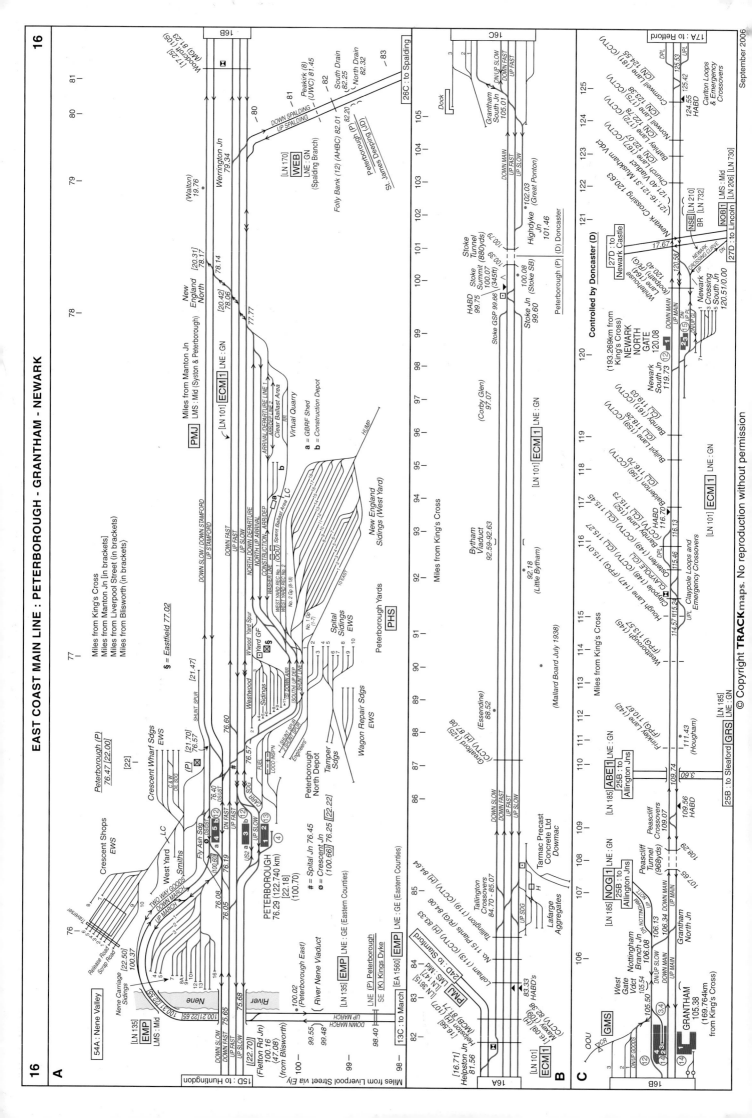

EAST COAST MAIN LINE : PETERBOROUGH - GRANTHAM - NEWARK

September 2006

© Copyright TRACKmaps. No reproduction without permission

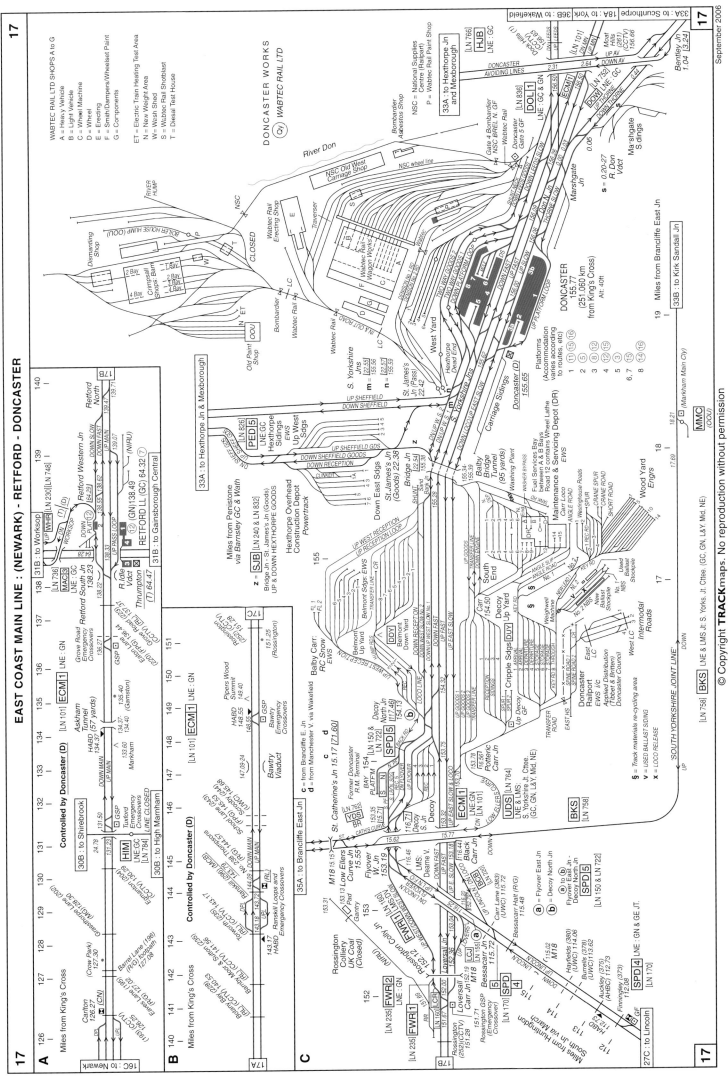

EAST COAST MAIN LINE : (NEWARK) - RETFORD - DONCASTER

© Copyright TRACKmaps. No reproduction without permission

September 2006

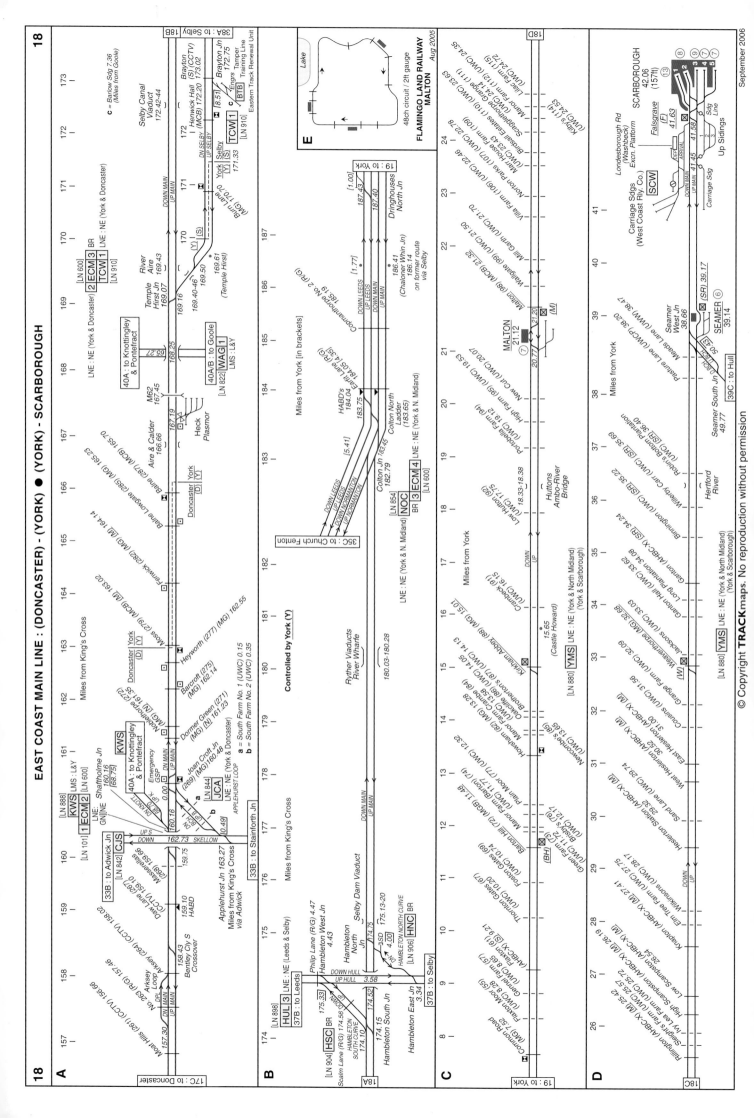

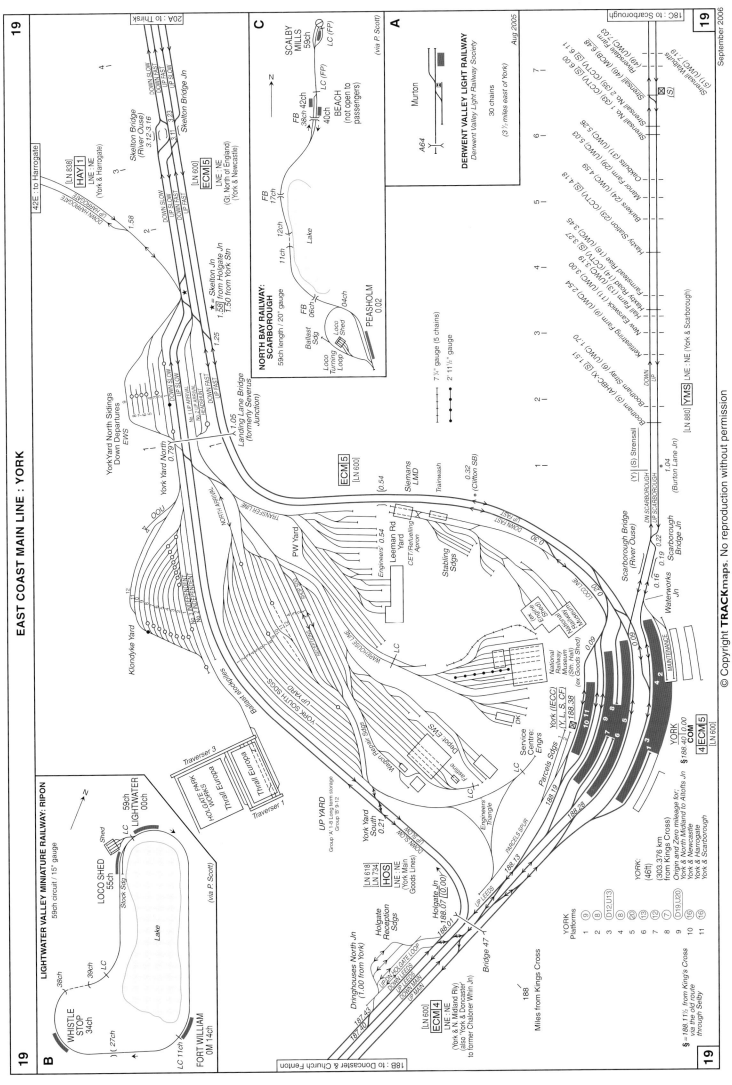

EAST COAST MAIN LINE : YORK

© Copyright TRACKmaps. No reproduction without permission

EAST COAST MAIN LINE : (YORK) - DARLINGTON - DURHAM

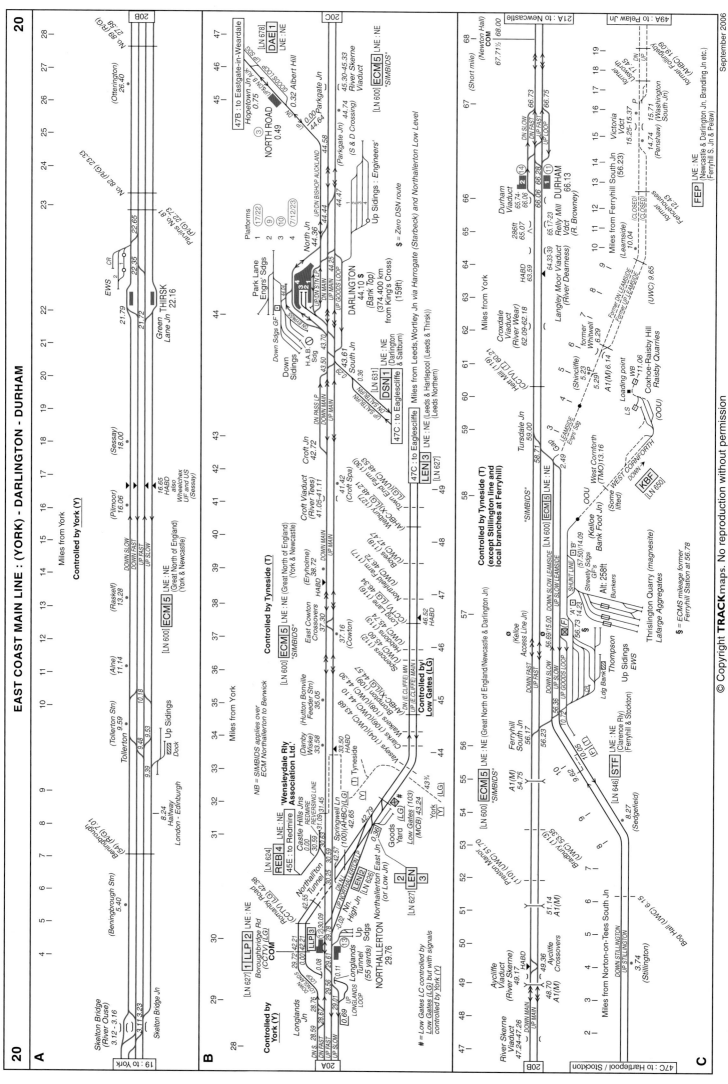

September 2006

EAST COAST MAIN LINE : CHESTER-LE-STREET - TYNE YARD ● LOW FELL - STOCKSFIELD

September 2006

EAST COAST MAIN LINE : NEWCASTLE - MORPETH - WIDDRINGTON

A

Heaton North Jn

2.70

Heaton GSP 2.35

Pile Sdg GF 2.55

Flushing Apron

2.58

Heaton Traction and Rolling Stock Maintenance Depot (HT) (Enlarged scale)

Maintenance Servicing Depot

Former Carriage Washing Shed

DOWN GOODS LOOP NORTH

WASHER LINE BY-PASS

DOWN GOODS LOOP SOUTH

DOWN MAIN

UP MAIN

UP GOODS LOOP

CW

No.4 SERVICE

HCS

DMU

FUEL

DEPOT ARRIVAL LINE

DEPOT DEPARTURE (1-9)

SPARE VEHICLE SDG A / SPARE VEHICLE SDG B

RECEPTION LINES (1-4)

STABLING 1-8

PRIMARY DEPARTURE (1-7)

HEATON CARRIAGE SDGS

Chillingham Rd 2.18

DEPOT ARRIVAL LINE 1.79

DEPOT DEPARTURE NECK

Heaton Carriage Sdgs Control Tower 1.65

Heaton South Jn 1.65

CT DEF.LINE 2.16

SIDINGS LINE

TYNE & WEAR METRO

WALKERGATE

52 : to Tynemouth

52

52

49A : to Sunderland

[LN 600] ECM 7 LNE : NE (Newcastle & Berwick) "SIMBIDS"

All lines controlled by Tyneside (T)

[LN 600] ECM 7 LNE : NE (Newcastle & Berwick)

Red Barns Jn

Argyle Tunnel St (98 yards)

MANORS 0.46

0.58

Dean St Crossover 0.40 (4)

Pilgrim St Crossover

Metro Tunnel

Viaduct

0.36

0.28

1.18 (Heaton)

1.04 1.25 (Riverside Jn)

0.56

Ouseburn Viaduct

1.51 (Heaton)

0.65-0.70

UP MAIN UP DN SLOW

DOWN MAIN

DOWN MAIN UP MAIN UP DN SLOW

LEN 3 LNE : NE (Newcastle & Berwick)

[LN 627] 101.46 101.31

High Level Bridge 1337ft long 112' high 101.49

GATESHEAD 100.40 Tyneside Central Freight Depot (OOU)

SHUNT SPUR

TIEE LINE

DOWN SUNDERLAND UP SUNDERLAND

St James' Bridge Jn 100.23

Park Lane Jn 100.65

Newcastle East Jn (Castles Jn) 101.59 0.14 0.11

NEWCASTLE 80.16 0.00

Platforms
1 (8)
2 (18)
3 (15)
4 (13)
5/6 (3/5/10)
7/8 (6/2/10)

120 ft

(432.323 km from King's Cross)

80.16 0.00

[LN 600] 6 ECM 7 [LN 600] LNE : NE (Newcastle & Berwick)

[LN 600] 5 ECM 6 LNE : NE (Newcastle & Carlisle) "SIMBIDS"

Newcastle West Jn 80.05 80.04 0.11

Newcastle South Jn 0.11

Viaduct 79.75

Viaduct 79.70

King Edward Bridge

King Edward Bridge North Jn 0.00

King Edward Bridge East Jn

King Edward Bridge South Jn 0.13

King Ed Br. S. Jn 0.62

SE CVE 0.00

Tyneside (IECC) (T) 0.32

[LN 676] HLK LNE : NE (G.N.&B.)

GATESHEAD 0.48 0.30 UP DN SLOW

GREENFIELDS WEST GREENFIELDS EAST

Greenfields Jn 0.21

High Street Jn 0.00 101.15

[LN 676] 2 PLG 1 LNE : NE

High Level Bridge Jn 0.00

High Level Bridge Central Jn 101.39

OAKWELL GATE SDG 101.33 101.31

Ø = [LN 620] KEB

* = [LN 674] HLK

W CURVE

Metro tunnel 0.27

Metro tunnel

(G.N.&B.) = Gateshead Norwood & Blaydon

[LN 674] HLK LNE : NE (G.N.&B.)

FORTH BANKS / PARADISE BRANCH

Elswick

1.02 1.00

0.51 DN Loop GF

0.25 0.22 arches

0.11

Castle Sdgs GF

Engrs Sdg OTM

Forth Banks Engineers Sdgs GF

1-29

[LN 662] NEN LNE : NE (Newcastle & Carlisle)

21B : to Durham / Carlisle

Askew Road Tunnel (53 yards) 79.26

Viaduct

79.53 79.49

79.42 79.29

79.66

0.48 0.64

UP MAIN DN MAIN UP CVE DOWN CARLISLE

UP FAST DOWN FAST UP SLOW DOWN SLOW

[LN 682] NEC 1 LNE : NE (G.N.&B.)

B

Miles from Newcastle

3 4 5 6 7 8 9 10 11 12 13 14 15 16 17 18 19 20 21 22 23 24 25

23A : to Alnmouth

Benton Crossovers 4.10

Benton (North) Jn 4.24 0.00 0.48 0.05

METRO UP B&T 0.64

Killingworth (CCTV) 4.57

Great Lime Road 5.50-5.53

52 : to Gosforth 4.41

52 : to Tynemouth

BLYTH & TYNE UP DOWN

23C : to Bedlington [LN 694] BNE LNE : NE

Killingworth Brideway 6.28

Dudley Brideway 7.73

Dam Dykes (CCTV) 8.46 8.45

HABD's

CRAMLINGTON 9.74 (5)

[LN 600] ECM 7 LNE : NE (Newcastle & Berwick) "SIMBIDS"

DOWN MAIN UP MAIN

Stannington (CCTV) 13.74

Clifton (CCTV) 14.36

Plessey Crossovers 11.51

Plessey (River Blyth) 12.17-23

Tyneside (T) Morpeth (M)

[LN 676] 2 PLG 1 LNE : NE

MORPETH 16.50

Morpeth 16.56 (M) 16.63 16.47

a

REV. SDG

BLYTH & TYNE DOWN

Morpeth North Jn 17.30 17.48-57 SD

Bothal (River Wansbeck) 17.30

Morpeth North (CCTV) 16.78

DOWN SLOW DOWN FAST UP FAST UP SLOW UP

Miles from Manors Jn via Percy Main

Miles from Leeds, Wortley Jn via Harrogate (Starbeck), Northallerton L.L. and Sunderland

PEGSWOOD 18.44 (4)

Controlled by Morpeth (M)

[LN 600] ECM 7 LNE : NE (Newcastle & Berwick) "SIMBIDS"

20.46 20.07 20.04 20.32

[LN 694] EJM BR

23C : to Ashington

Signal B6 (NR) 5.38 SOUTH BRANCH [LN 698]

0.00

[0.71] 0.00

Butterwell Jn 20.63 20.52

Ughpen Garage (CCTV) 23.23 23.24

Longhirst (CCTV) 20.17

BWO

Butterwell Disposal Point UK Coal

Butterwell (B) "SIMBIDS"

GF 'A' GF 'C' WB

NR Bdy

Fireclay Loading Pad

NORTH BRANCH [LN 700]

z x y

BUNKER LINE

DOWN

Ughpen Garage (CCTV) 23.20

WIDDRINGTON 23.20 (4)

Widdrington Opencast Disposal Point UK Coal

Felton Lane (CCTV) 25.16

24.63

Widdrington Sdgs 24.60

Exchange Sdgs

Tare WB LS

Gross WB

Screens

c ½ mile

x = Signal box for working to Ashington
y = Large coal bunker
z = Rapid loading bunker

Mileages in [brackets] are Light Railway Order mileages

a = Coopies Lane 20.40 (AHBC)
b = Barmoor through siding (No.2)
c = Electrification Depot

Parkside Farm 19.38

Hepscott Jn 19.44

Freight Sdgs EWS [LN 696] HJM

[LN 694] EJM LNE : NE (Blyth & Tyne)

23C : to Bedlington

Bermoor N. Side DOWN 20.47

REV. SDG

September 2006

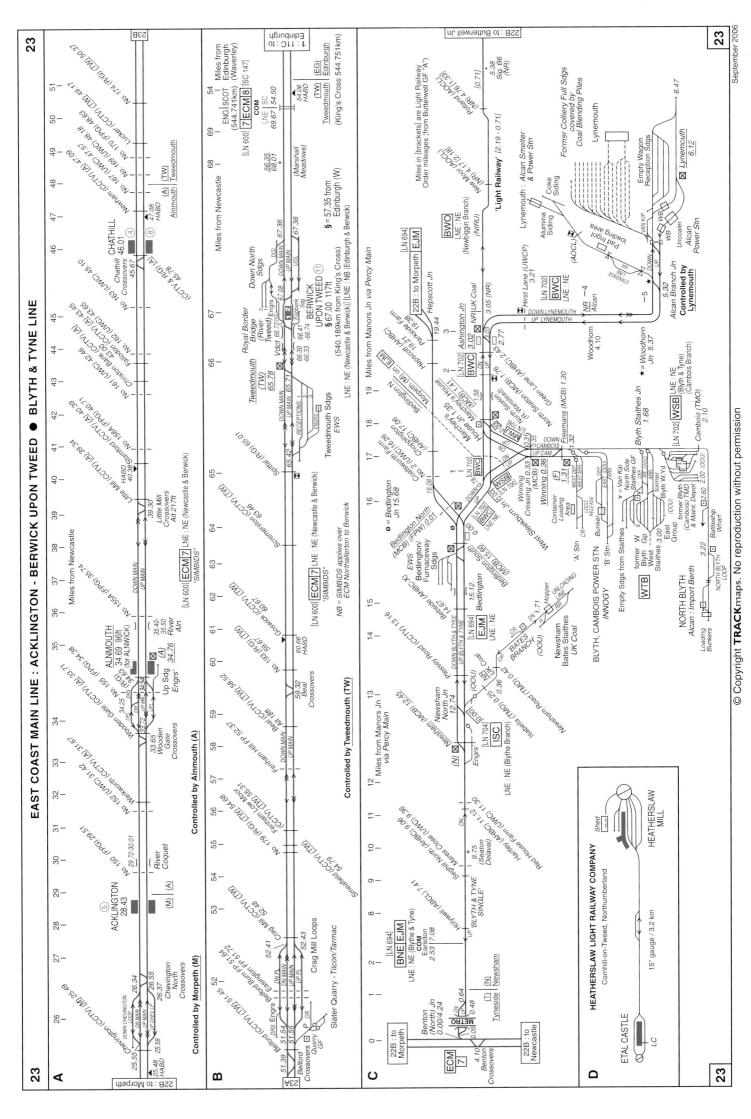

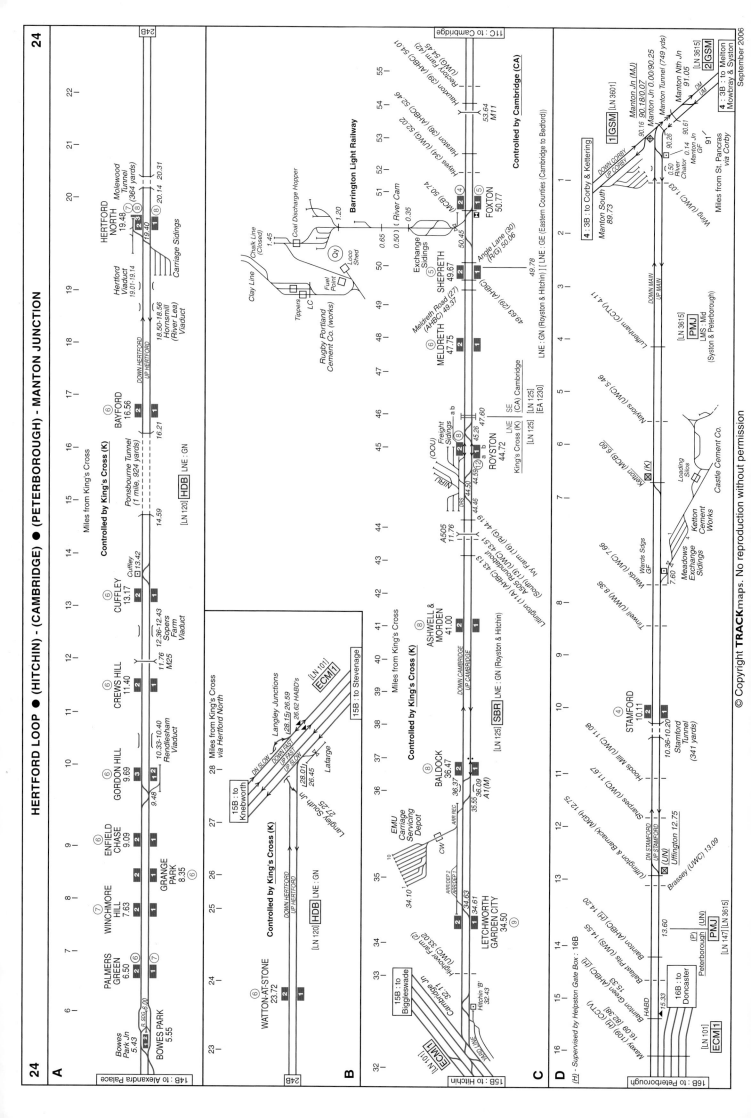

© Copyright **TRACK**maps. No reproduction without permission

September 2006

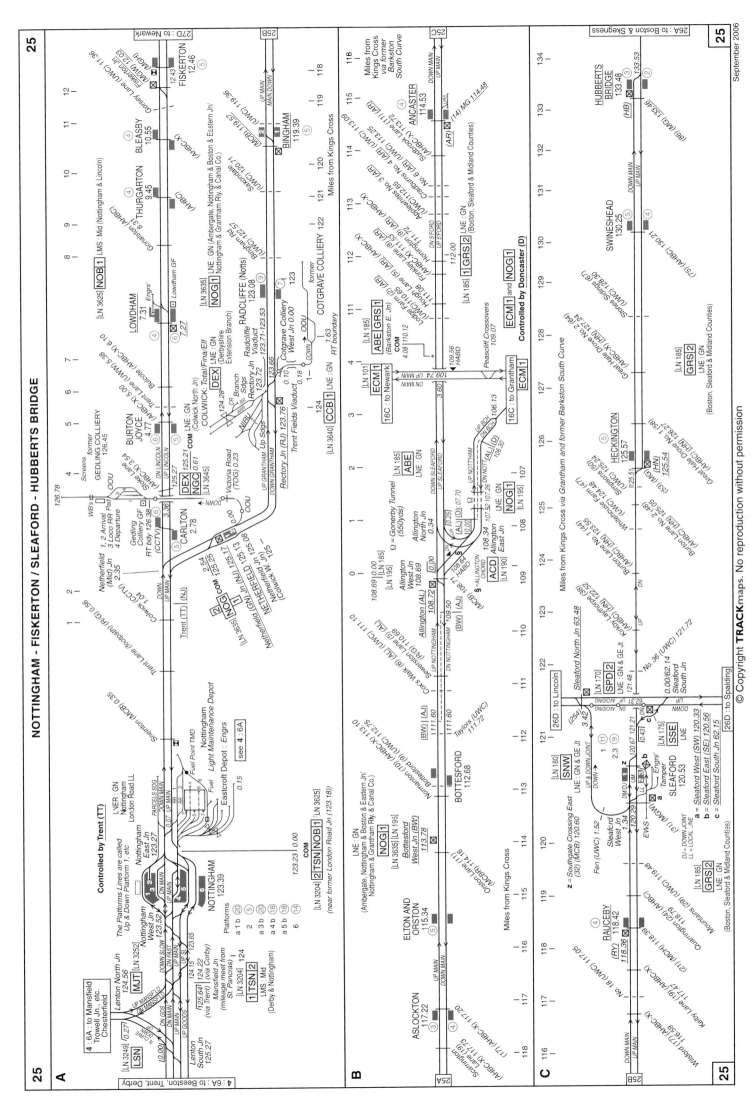

NOTTINGHAM - FISKERTON / SLEAFORD - HUBBERTS BRIDGE

September 2006

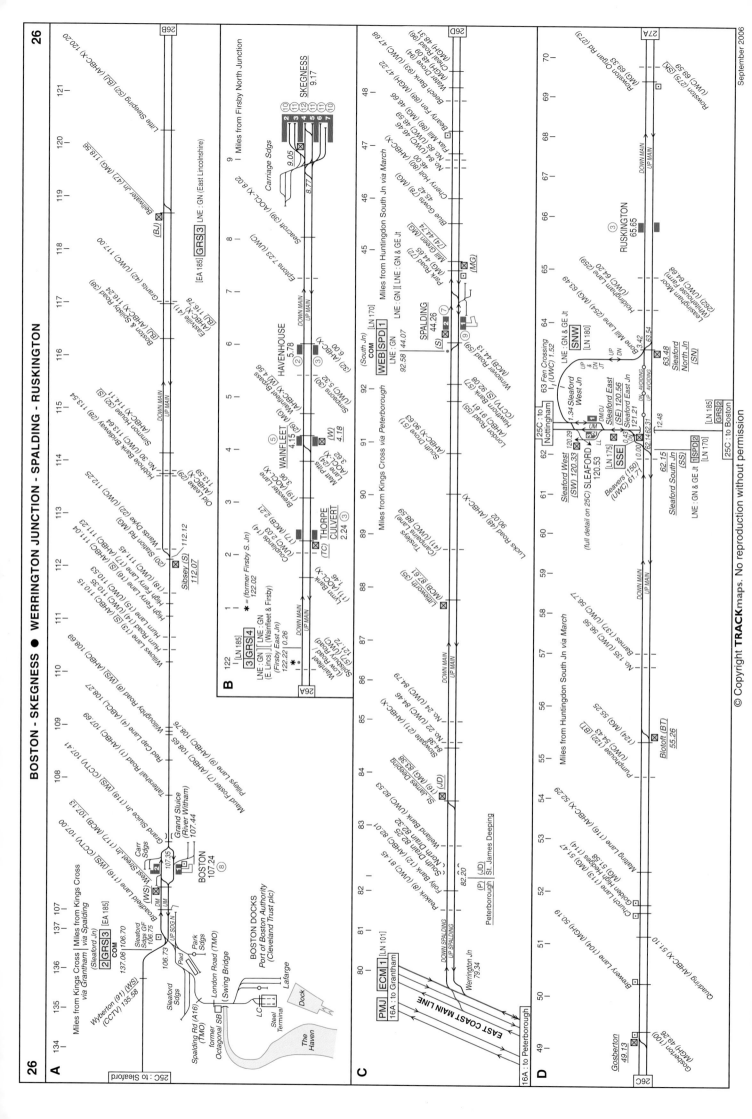

BOSTON - SKEGNESS ● WERRINGTON JUNCTION - SPALDING - RUSKINGTON

September 2006

METHERINGHAM - LINCOLN - GAINSBOROUGH - (DONCASTER) ● FISKERTON - LINCOLN

A

Miles from Huntingdon South Jn via March

27E : to Newark Castle 84

[LN 206 & LN 730] NOB 2
BR (deviation)

(0.00)/32.40 Boultham Jn
Pyewipe Jn 84.13
BHP
(0.65)
NEWARK LNE : GN & GE Jt MCBW1 DOWN NEWARK UP NEWARK PYEWIPE
[LN 170] SPD 3
LNE : GN
West Holmes (WH) 83.29

138.13 from KX via Boston
(PS) = (41.26 from New Holland)
High Street (154) (MCB) 82.49
Brayford (155) (CCTV) 82.57
DOWN MAIN UP MAIN DOWN GOODS UP GOODS 32.70
Ruston's Tip (R/G) 32.52
East Holmes 82.60

Platforms 3 ⑤ 4 ③ 6.7 ⑦
⑤ ⑥ ⑧ ⑦ 5 4 3
Pelham Street (PS) 82.29
LNE : GN & GE Jt LNE : GN
LINCOLN 82.41 LNE : GN (Central)
Sincil Bank (CCTV) 82.19
DOWN UP 82.31
27E : to Wrawby Jn

European Metal Recycling
Terrace Sidings (former Washingborough Branch, LNE : GN) 137.67
2 SPD 3 [LN 170]
(Greetwell Jn)
81.25

Branston & Washingborough Cross Roads Tunnel (60yds)
79.44-79.47

Howards (295) (UWC) 75.70

SPD 2 [LN 170]
LNE : GN & GE Jt

Ox Pasture Lane (292) (FPd) 73.62
Robinsons (291) (MG)
Blankney Moor (Lane) (287)
Martin Road (283) (UWC) 73.09
Blankney Estates (285) (UWC) 72.44
METHERINGHAM 73.03
③ DS US
Timberland Rd (MG) Scopwick (278) 70.48
(SK)

26D : to Peterborough

B

27C

Walkeringham Misterton : British Pipeline Agency Qv
103.65
Tetheringfass Lane (UWC) 101.54
Masons Lane (348) 100.78
Walkeringham (353) (UWC) 102.52
Gainsborough Rd (322) (UWC) 100.06
EGF Beckingham (B)
[LN 170] SPD 4 LNE : GN & GE Jt
Beckingham 83.29 UGL (NIRU) EGF (NIRU)

DOWN MAIN UP MAIN
[LN 736] MAC 3
31B : to Retford
Gainsborough Trent Jn 73.24/98.56
HABD 98.56
Trent West Jn 98.87
Trent East Jn 73.22 73.14/98.58-98.66
River Trent 73.24/98.56
MAC 3 [LN 736]
DOCK WHARF LC Ldg Gantry
GAINSBOROUGH LEA ROAD 98.09
⑦ 98.03
Gainsborough Oil Terminal Pentex Melrose Oil & Gas

Miles from Huntingdon South Jn via March

Foxes (329) (UWC) 95.35
Hansons (327) (UWC) 95.08 (SP)
[LN 170] SPD 3 LNE : GN & GE Jt
Stow Park Tillbridge Lane (326) 93.13 (MG) (SP)

89.15 (GW)
DOWN MAIN UP MAIN
Sykes Lane (318) (UWC)
SAXILBY 88.51
Saxilby 88.41 West Bank (MG)
No. 316 (UWC) 88.75
Hockings (314) (UWC) 88.57
Fossdyke Navigation Canal 88.38

(B) Beckingham (D) Doncaster
River Bank (305) (UWMD) 87.04
Keyeven (307) (AHBC-X) 87.41

27A

C 104

Miles from Huntingdon South Jn via March

Controlled by Doncaster (D)

27E
Langholt (341) (AHBC) 20.24
Winthorpe (109) (AHBC) 19.01
20.24 HABD
DOWN MAIN UP MAIN
[LN 210 & LN 732] NSE BR
Newark Crossing South Jn 120.51/0.00
NEWARK CROSSING CURVE
Newark Cross'g E. Jn 117.67/120.63
DOWN MAIN UP MAIN
Newark Cranley Point 17.7/6
Miles from Nottingham (London Road Jn)

ECM 1 [LN 101]
16C : to Retford
16C : to Gainsborough Central (via Newark North Gate)
16C : to Grantham
Newark Crossing 17.67/120.63
River Devon Viaduct 17.51-17.59
31B : to Gainsborough Central and Cleethorpes
MAC 3 [LN 736]

16.02
NEWARK CASTLE (NC) 17.00
(MCB) 16.78 17.02
P4 ④ 1 ③
Tolney Lane Vdct 17.00
(SC) (NC)
Old Trent Dyke Vdct 15.79- 15.35
Averham Weir Vdct 16.02
a b c d
a = Arnolds Flood Bridge 14.49-14.51
b = Weightmans Viaduct 15.04-15.06
c d = Flood openings 15.53-15.55
15.21- 15.35
15.43-15.46

NOB 1 LMS : Mid (Nottingham & Lincoln)
[LN 3625] [LN 730]
[LN 206]
(SC)
Starthorpe Crossing (MCB) 14.20
Brettles (UWC) 13.67
Rolleston Mill (UWC) 13.24
ROLLESTON 13.13 ⑦
FISKERTON 12.46 ⑤
(M&W) 13.08
(M&W) 12.43

D
25A : to Nottingham
17C : to Doncaster

RAF Finningley = Robin Hood International Airport)
Finningley (37) (MCB) 112.08
112
Woodland (37) (CCTV) 111.53
DOWN LINCOLN UP LINCOLN
Beech Hill (368) (AHBC) 110.73
Park Drain (365) (CCTV) 108.52
Brornston (364) (UWC) 108.13
Park Drain (365) 108.13
[LN 170] SPD 4 LNE : GN & GE Jt
Haxey & Epworth 106.24
Haxey (359) (CCTV) 105.58
Tindall (358) (UWC) 104.66
North Carr (MG) River Bank (305)
Kesteven (307) (AHBC-X)

27B

E

27 28A : to Wrawby Jn

Miles from New Holland
Spa Street (71) (UWC) 40.42
Sidings
Sincil Bank (CCTV) 82.19
[LN 206 & LN 730] NOB 3 LNE : GC (Great Grimsby & Sheffield Jn)
Pelham Street 82.29
High Street (154) (MCB) 82.49 [LN 170] SPD 3
Brayford (155) (CCTV) 82.57
LINCOLN 82.41 LNE : GN (Central)
East Holmes 82.60
⑤ ③ 5
④ ⑦ 4
⑤ ⑥ ⑦ DOWN UP 41.26
Pyewipe Jn 84.13 West Holmes (WH) 83.29
27A : to Spalding

27A : to Gainsborough
SPD 3 [LN 170]
DOWN UP
Boultham
BHP (0.65) DN 0.00
1 NOB 2 BR (deviation)
LMS : Mid (Nottingham & Lincoln)
[LN 206 & LN 730]
Ruston's Tip (R/G) 32.52
32.40 DOWN UP
Miles from Huntingdon South Jn via March
Boultham Crossing (CCTV) 31.17
Doddington Road (CCTV) (MCB) 30.18
HYKEHAM 29.44 ④
(63A) (AHBC-X)
Thorpe-on-the-Hill (60A) (UWC) 27.75
Whisby Quarry (62) 27.28
Walkers (63) (UWC) 28.50
(WH) West Holmes
(S) Swinderby West Holmes
Thorpe (AHBC) 26.53
Eagle Barnsdale (56A) (AHBC) 25.54
Eagle & Thorpe (AHBC) 24.67
[LN 206 & LN 730] NOB 1
LMS : Mid (Nottingham & Lincoln)
(S) 24.68
③ ④
SWINDERBY 24.64
Meadhall (59) (MG) 24.31
South Scarle (55A) (AHBC) 24.31
Clemens No. 1 (52)
Tillings (51) (UWC) 23.49
Swinderby Road (48B) 22.34
Cross Lane (48B) 22.46
Westerbrook Lane (48A) (AHBC) 21.44
Cottage Lane (45A) (AHBC) 21.16
COLLINGHAM 22.17 ②
22.02 (S) Swinderby
(D) Doncaster | Swinderby

27D

September 2006

© Copyright TRACKmaps. No reproduction without permission

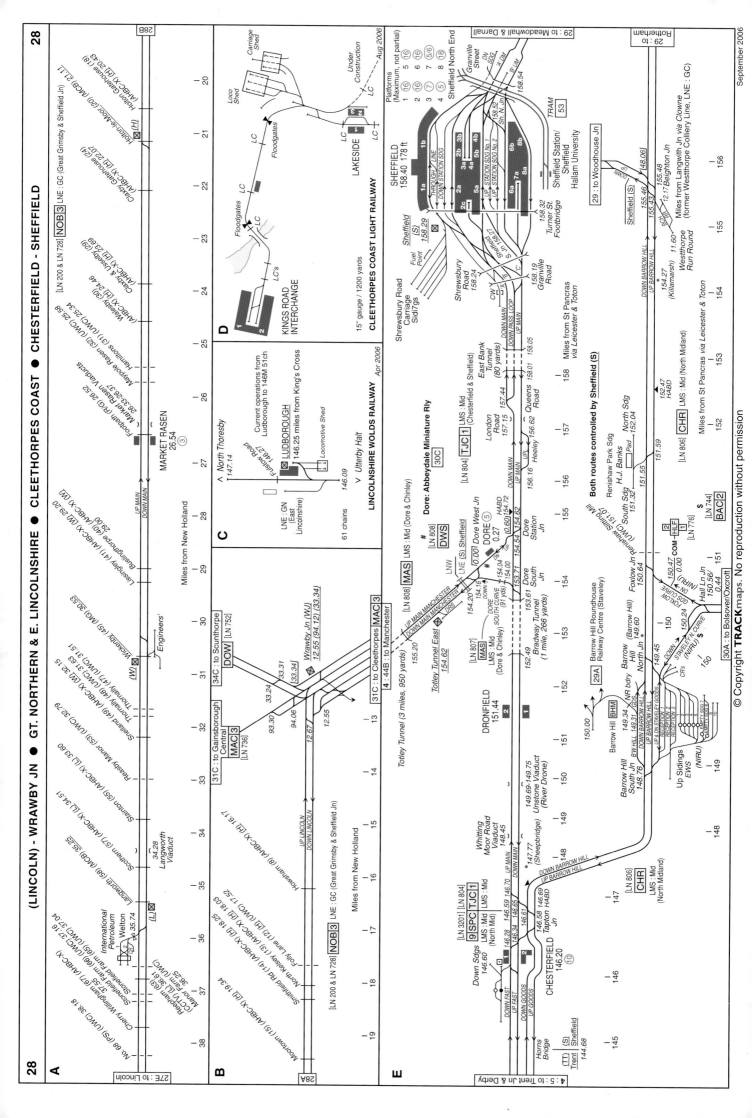

(LINCOLN) - WRAWBY JN ● GT. NORTHERN & E. LINCOLNSHIRE ● CLEETHORPES COAST ● CHESTERFIELD - SHEFFIELD

September 2006

(SHEFFIELD) - MEADOWHALL - ROTHERHAM ● (SHEFFIELD) - WOODHOUSE ● TINSLEY YARD

A BARROW HILL ROUNDHOUSE RAILWAY CENTRE (Staveley)

Springwell Branch
Up crossing 148.60
Up occupation crossing 148.82
150.00
149.63 (Mileage reversal point for running line) (Aug 2006)

28E
[BHM] Connecting Line
NR 3dy 145.34

Proposed Storage Sdgs
Whittington Road (Up) Running Road
UP Preparation Pit Rd
Coal Road
Ash Pit Rd - Front Rd
Storage Rds
Running Line
Loop

Deltic Preservation 1
Society Depot 2
Commercial Roads 2
Van Roads 2
Garden Rd
Roundhouse contains 24 rds all with pits
Loading/Unloading Area
ROUNDHOUSE HALT 150.04

B CLEETHORPES: PLEASURE ISLAND RAILWAY
2' gauge / 37th circuit
via P. Scott
Lake
Tunnel/Shed
LC

M1 159.43
Up Canklow Loop 160.11
Up Barrow Hill
Down Barrow Hill
Canklow 160

[TNC] (TY)
Catcliffe Jn 159.15
Catcliffe Viaduct
Treeton
159.23 159.19
DN GDS LINE
See Near Dep (DN)
See Far Dep (Up)
(TY)
[BTJ]
159.58

(Treeton North Jn) 159.19 —159
Treeton Jn 158.65 —158
Woodhouse Mill Jn 157.37 —157
31A : to Worksop

Masborough Sorting Sidings South Jn 160.57
160.61
FL1
Crane Rd
HH SHUNT NECK
Rotherham Masborough
Tarmac Coating & Concrete Plants
Pad
159.76
[BTJ] [LN 809]
LNE : Sheffield District

EAST DEPARTURE
EAST ARRIVAL
MAIN YARD
M.YD NECK
160.07
E.DEP
SECONDARY YARD EAST DEP
(TY) Tinsley Yard 160.02

River Rother Viaduct 47.02-47.06
47
Viaduct 47.15-47.20
Woodhouse Mill 47.22
156.44

[LN 736] [MAC]3 LNE : GC (Sheffield & Lincolnshire Jn. Rly)
[CHR] LMS : Mid (Nth. Midland) —156
[LN 806]
Beighton Jn 48.05
Beighton Stn. Jn 47.42
155.46 48.08
155.43 Westthorpe Run Round 11.60
Beighton Engineering Sdgs : Edgar Allen
[BX]
(S) Sheffield
NIRU
[LN 816] [BEW] LNE : GC
28E: to Chesterfield

Shepcote Lane New Sdgs
Tinsley : Avesta SPACE (Stainless Plate And Coil Expansion) OUTOKUMPU
[CHR] [LN 806] LMS : Mid (North Midland) —161
Miles from St Pancras via Leicester, Toton & Treeton

UP
EAST ARRIVAL
EAST DEPARTURE
160.52
TINSLEY YARD : EWS (former Main Yard)
Tinsley Park 160.68
Tinsley Avesta (TMO) 161.04
WEST DEPARTURE / ARRIVAL

Tinsley Park
Avesta SMACC (Stainless Melting And Continuous Casting) OUTOKUMPU
NR boundary
46
45
44
43
Miles from Manchester (London Road) via Woodhead
UP WORKSOP
DOWN WORKSOP
DARNALL 43.23
Woodhouse Jn 46.52
46.56
WOODHOUSE 46.18
(WH)

[LN 809] [SEL] BR
S
[LN 810]
Shepcote Lane W. Jn (W) 161.23
Tinsley East Jn 3 2.79
Tinsley South Jn 2.22 161.63 M12.38
Shepcote Lane East Jn 161.20
161.12 161.63 (TY) S
161.67
Broughton Lane Jn 1.36
[LN 812] [BLJ] BR
Controlled by Wooburn Jn (W)
WEST CURVE
SW CURVE

Miles from St Pancras via Leicester, Toton & Sheffield
[WME] [LN 830] LNE : GC
42.40
Wooburn Jn 42.29
42.22 Tram over (see 53)
(W)
0.56 (Attercliffe)
0.00
ATTERCLIFFE ROAD 159.34
42.40
[NUJ]2 [LN 736] BR/LMS : LNW
Nunnery Jn 41.68 159.33
Nunnery Main Line 158.77
158.67 158.60
Sheffield (S)
28E : to Sheffield

33A : to Swinton & Mexborough via Aldwarke Jn
[LN 830] [WME] LNE : GC (South Yorks & River Don)
6 Miles from Woodburn Jn —5

Controlled by Sheffield (S)
ROTHERHAM CENTRAL 4.60
[LN 818] [HCD] BR
Rotherham Central Jn 4.40
Rotherham Main (UWC) 4.01 —4

161 Miles from St Pancras via Leicester, Toton and Barrow Hill

161.40 161.28 Ickles Viaduct
161.45 4.00
UP TINSLEY
DOWN TINSLEY

—164 —163
Millmoor C F Booth
[WBH] LMS : Mid (Sheffield & Rotherham) 0.62
Westgate Sdg
Up B. Hill 161.66
162.18 0.20
Holmes Jn (CCTV) (0.00)
Sheffield (S) / Wooburn Jn (W)

Brinsworth St
Holmes Curve 0.36

53 TRAM
Meadowhall Interchange
M1 (Tinsley Vdct) 162.16
MEADOWHALL INTERCHANGE 161.70
Wincobank Jn 161.52
BRIGHTSIDE 161.27 —162
Brightside Loop
Brightside Stn. Jn 161.12 —161
Mill Race Jn 160.18 —160
159.65
Valley Centertainment
Arena
Stocksbridge

ROTHERHAM MASBOROUGH 162.00
[TJC]3 [LN 804] LMS : Mid (North Midland)
Masborough (Station) Jn 162.24
Miles from St Pancras via Leicester, Toton & Barrow Hill
[TJC]2 161.77 163.74 Holmes Lane Sdg
[TJC]3
[LN 804]
Masborough (Masborough Stn. Stn. Jn)

Up Barnsley 162.00
Dn Barnsley
163.43
Wincobank Vdct 161.70
Down Main / Up Main
UP & DN SLOW
Up & Dn Goods
No 1 REC
UM / DM
41.12 41.39 41.48
160.34 [LN 804]
LMS : Mid
—38 (Grimesthorpe Jn)
Brightside Stn. Jn 161.12 —36 —37
LMS : Mid (Sheffield & Rotherham) —35 —34

Controlled by Barnsley (BY)
Miles from St Pancras via Leicester, Toton & Sheffield via Barnsley
Chapeltown Viaduct 165.63
[TJC] 166.28
Tankersley Tunnel (1498 yds)
35D : to Barnsley

164 165 166
UP MAIN / DOWN MAIN
Up Barnsley (BY) / Sheffield (S)
Dn Barnsley
162.14

Ecclesfield Emergency Operating Panel 164.09
Butterthwaite Lane (UWC) 164.61
Ellencliffe Loop
Exchange Sdgs
Deepcar
Deepcar Viaduct (River Don) 33.35 33.20 NR bdy
Stocksbridge Engineering Steels
United Engineering Steels
[SKL] Stocksbridge Light Railway 0.00 - 2.07
LS
[SHB] [LN 868] LMS : Mid / BR
Butterthwaite Lane (UWC) (Stairfoot)
CHAPELTOWN 165.68

STOCKSBRIDGE LINE
[MAC]3 [LN 750] LNE : GC (Sheffield, Ashton-under-Lyne and Manchester Railway)
Miles from Manchester (London Road) via Woodhead
WADSLEY BRIDGE
Wadsley Viaduct 38.77 —39
38.36 38.35
Victoria Vdct arches 1-42 159.17 159.01
Victoria Viaduct 41.22 41.12 41.39 41.48
Broad Street Tunnel (109 yards) 158.76
Miles from St Pancras via Leicester, Toton & Sheffield
Sheffield (S)
(Tram over)
41.12 (Sheffield) 41.22 (Victoria)
LMS : Mid

—40
(TJC) 2
[LN 804]
RR / A / B

© Copyright TRACKmaps. No reproduction without permission

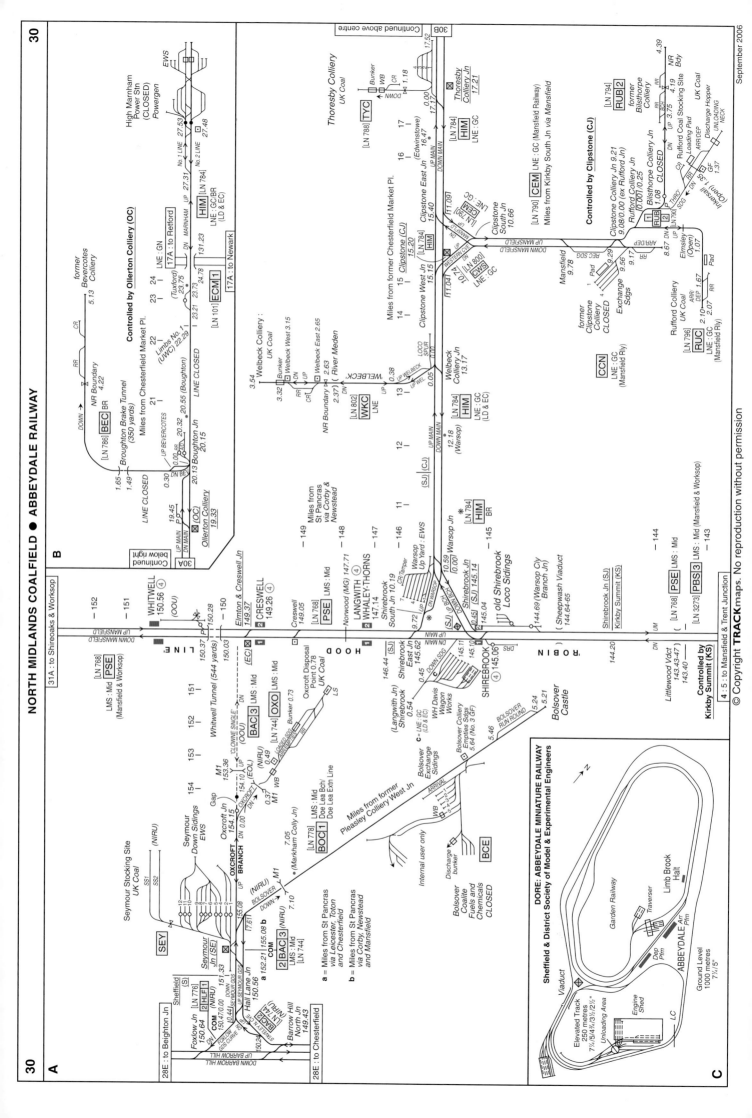

NORTH MIDLANDS COALFIELD ● ABBEYDALE RAILWAY

KIVETON BRIDGE - WORKSOP - RETFORD - GAINSBOROUGH - BARNETBY

A

29 : to Rotherham

CHR [LN 806] LMS : Mid (North Midland)

29 : to Beighton Jn [LN 806]

29 : to Sheffield

156.44
47.22

M1
49.28

Miles from Manchester (London Road) via Woodhead

[LN 736] MAC3 LNE : GC (Sheffield & Lincolnshire Jn)

UP MAIN
DOWN MAIN

KIVETON BRIDGE 50.34

Rapid Loading Pad former Kiveton Park Colliery UK Coal

OOU 50.70

KIVETON PARK 51.50

Thorpe Salvin Bridleway 52.21

(MOB) 51.52

(KS)

35A : to Doncaster

BKS [LN 758]

52.40

Brancliffe East Jn 53.57

UP SY SOUTH YORKSHIRE
DOWN SY 10.00

Wood Yard 54.56

(WP) 54.56

Shireoaks West Jn 55.00/154.36

SHIREOAKS 54.52 ⑤

SHW LMS : Mid
Worksop (WP) LMS : Mid

PSE [LN 782] LMS : Mid (Mansfield & Worksop)

[LN 768]

30A : to Shirebrook

Shireoaks East Jn 55.62

Woodend Jn 153.70

UP MANSFIELD
DOWN MANSFIELD
WEST GDS CURVE
WN

153

Miles from St Pancras via Corby & Newstead

Rockware Glass

Worksop Up Yard

16 15 10

SN
GN REP 2 UP REP 1
UP REP 2
SN DEP · FAR DN RECEPTION 1
UP DEP No. 2
UP DEP No. 1
Up Rec 2 also RR

Worksop (WP) 56.55 ⑥

Worksop West Jn

WORKSOP 56.61 ⑥

Worksop East (CCTV) (WP) 56.64

LOCO SDG
UP MAIN
DOWN MAIN

Freight Sdgs EWS

Merry-go-round Repair Depot W.H. DAVIS & Son

Worksop Down Yard EWS

DN DEP · FAR DN RECEPTION 1
DN RECEPTION 2

31B

[LN 736] MAC3 LNE : GC (Sheffield & Lincolnshire Jn)

Manton Wood (or Manton Colliery) Jn 58.54

Manton Wood Sdg

River Ryton Viaduct & Chesterfield Canal 58.30-36 (WP)

48 49 50 51 52 53 54 55 56 57 58 59 60

B

(WP) Worksop

UP MAIN
DOWN MAIN

Mansfield Rd (CCTV) (T)

Rushey Sdgs (AHBC-X) 62.45

(T) Thrumpton

[LN 230] WHR LNE : GC
[LN 748]

Retford Western Jn 64.24/138.55

Doncaster (D) LNE : GC (T)

63.28

Thrumpton West Jns (Whisker Hill) 63.46

63.74 64.20

DN WORKSOP
UP WORKSOP
SDT
DOWN GN
UP GN

17A : to Doncaster

RETFORD 138.49 (GN) ⑫ 64.32 (GC) ⑦

(GC) Gringley Rd UGL (T)

Gringley Road (RC) 65.15

Thrumpton (MCB) 64.47

138.33
138.62 DN FAST
138.22 DOWN PLAT
Retford South 138.23
River Idle Vdct

17A : to Newark LNE : GN

ECM1 [LN 101]

UP PASSENGER LOOP
UP MAIN

Miles from Manchester (London Road) via Woodhead

[LN 736] MAC3 LNE : GC (Sheffield & Lincolnshire Jn)

Chequerhouse (UWC) 67.33
Rat Hole Lane (T)

Clarborough Tunnel (658 yds)

Clarborough Jn 68.32

Windmill Lane (UWC) 69.05
67.49·70 (UWC)

Freemans Lane (UWC) 69.60

West Burton West Jn 70.66

West Burton (WB) 71.40

(T) WB

Westbrecks (AHBC-X) 71.22
Leverton (AHBC-X) 70.16

UP BCH
DN BCH

EGF

TYB1 [LN 746] LNE : GC (Sheffield & Lincolnshire Extn. Rly)

Cripple Sdg (EWS)

Coal Hoppers

Inwards Coal Line

CPS [LN 746]

Cottam Power Station : London Power

West GF

WEST REC 1
W. REP No.1

West Burton Jn 72.07
E. DEP 1

WBC BR

West Burton Power Station London Power $

C Coal
D Lines
E Dust
F Lines
H WB
Oil
K
L
LS
Ash Pits

EAST REC
Giggles Repair Yd
E DEP

Oil Gantries
★ Flyash Dust Hoppers
$ Coal Plant Control Room

Bole (UWC) 72.18

West Burton East Jn 72.20
E East GF 72.18

Oil Discharge

Emergency Coal Discharge

HABD 73.24 DN 98.66-58
73.14-22

Trent W. Jn 73.12

Trent Jn 73.24 98.56

River Trent 98.55

Trent E. Jn ⊠ (GC) 74.33
74.42

[LN 170]

SPD4 [LN 736] MAC3 LNE : GC (Great Grimsby & Sheffield Jn)

GAINSBOROUGH CENTRAL ⑦

74.42
74.36 (GC)

27B : to Gainsborough Lea Road and Lincoln

SPD3 [LN 170]

31C

27B : to Doncaster

61 62 63 64 65 66 67 68 69 70 71 72 73 74

C

⑦ GAINSBOROUGH CENTRAL

74.42
74.36 (GC)

76.061

Thonock Lane Farm (UWC) 76.39

Miles from Manchester (London Road) via Woodhead

(GC)

Bonsall Lane 80.23

Swinedyke 81.38
82.14 (MG)
82.17 (GW)

Northorpe (N)

DOWN\UP LOOP

82.67

Kettleby (AHBC) (W) 92.58

Hibaldstow (AHBC-X) 89.03

KIRTON LINDSEY ⑥
84.65
85.10

Kirton Tunnel (1334 yards)

Kirton Lime Sdgs (KL) 86.20
85.72

BRIGG (MG) ⑦
91.01
Brigg (B) 91.23

[LN 736] MAC3 LNE : GC (Great Grimsby & Sheffield Jn)

Wrawby Jn (33,34) 94.12
(12.55) (WJ)
33.31 ⊠ (WJ) 94.06

34C : to Scunthorpe

DOW [LN 752]

NOB3 [LN 200]
[LN 728]

28B : to Lincoln

33.24
33.34
93.30
94.06
94.35
94.56 (WL)

Hibaldstow (AHBC-X) 89.03

New Barnetby (4) (MG) 95.1

BARNETBY (for Humberside Airport) 94.56

1 2
3 4

Barnetby East ⊠ (BE) 94.64

UP GOODS
UP SLOW
UP FAST
DOWN FAST
DOWN SLOW
DOWN GOODS

Up Sidings
Down Sdgs

ENGINEERS
No. 1 RECEPTION
No. 2 RECEPTION

DEAD END
LINCOLN

CR

32A : to Cleethorpes

31A 31B

75 76 77 78 79 80 81 82 83 84 85 86 87 88 89 90 91 92 93 94 95 96

September 2006

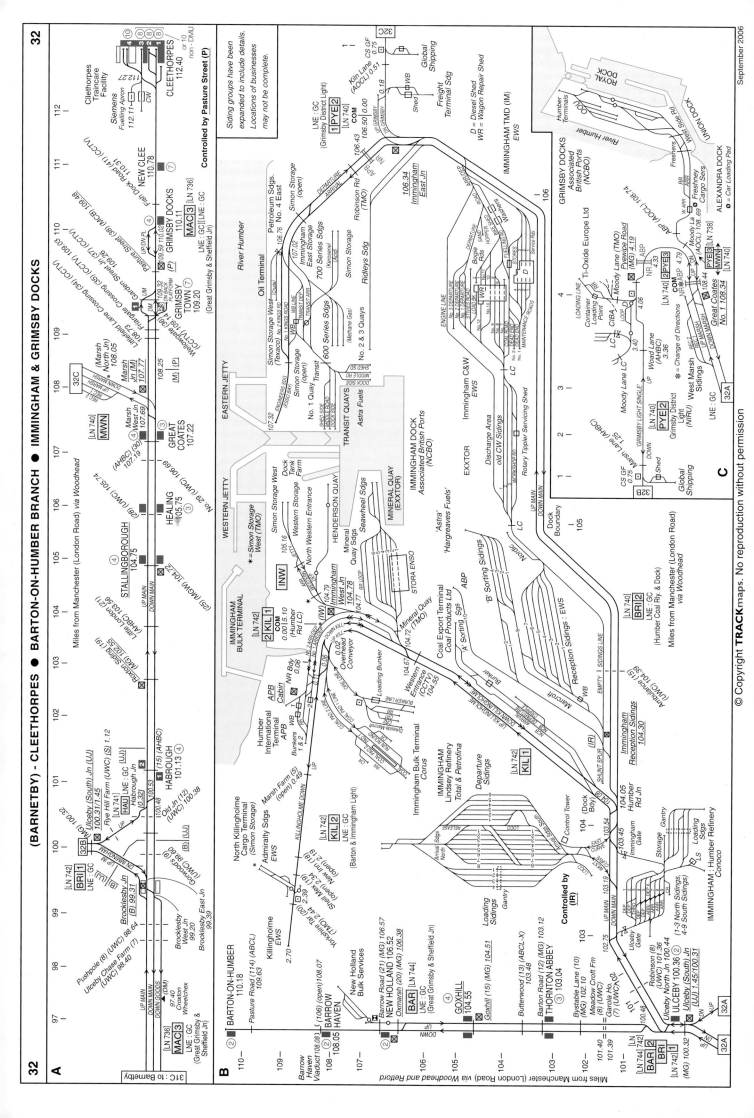

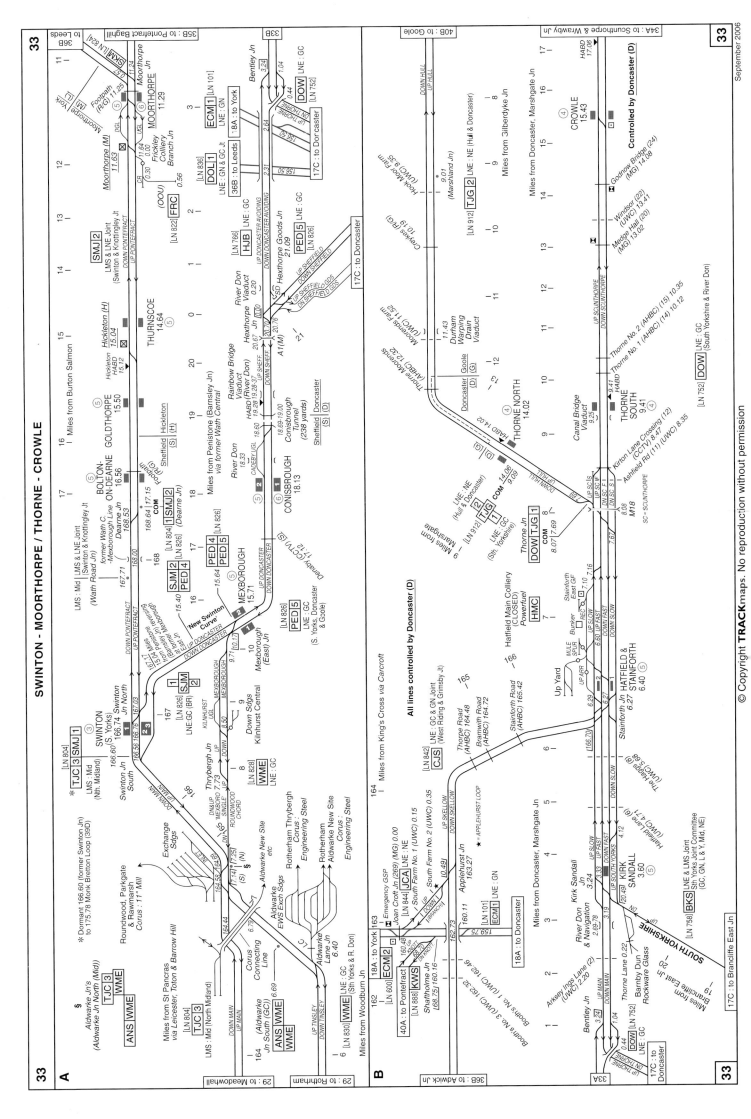

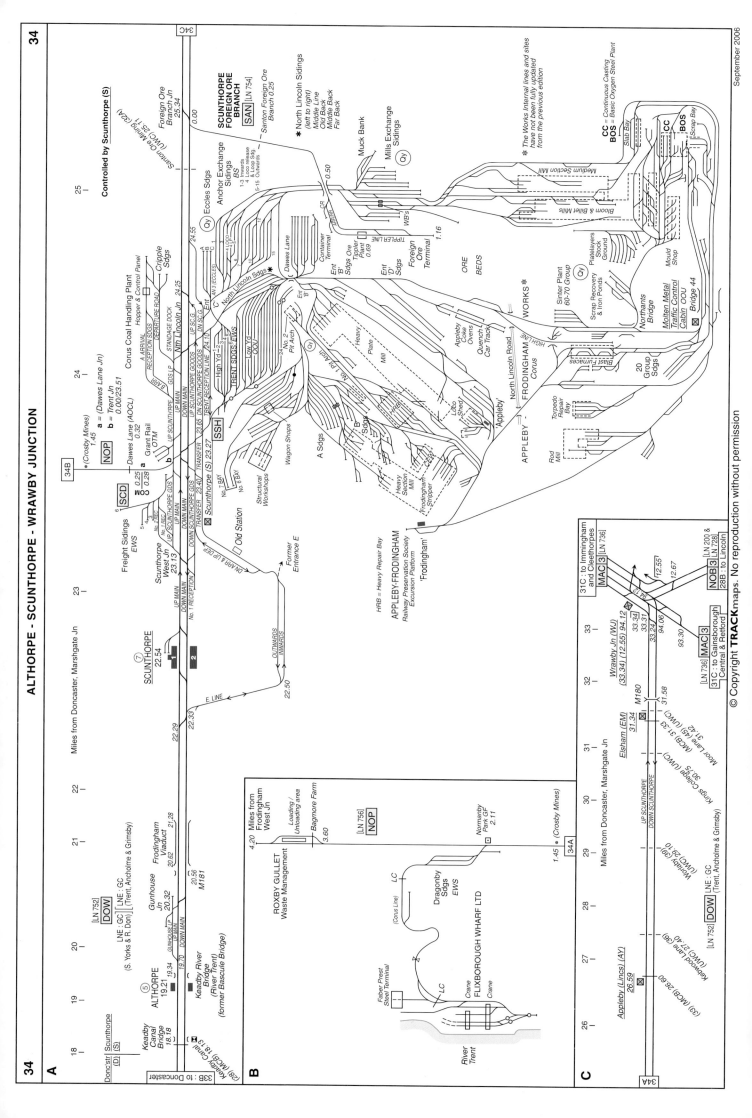

ALTHORPE - SCUNTHORPE - WRAWBY JUNCTION

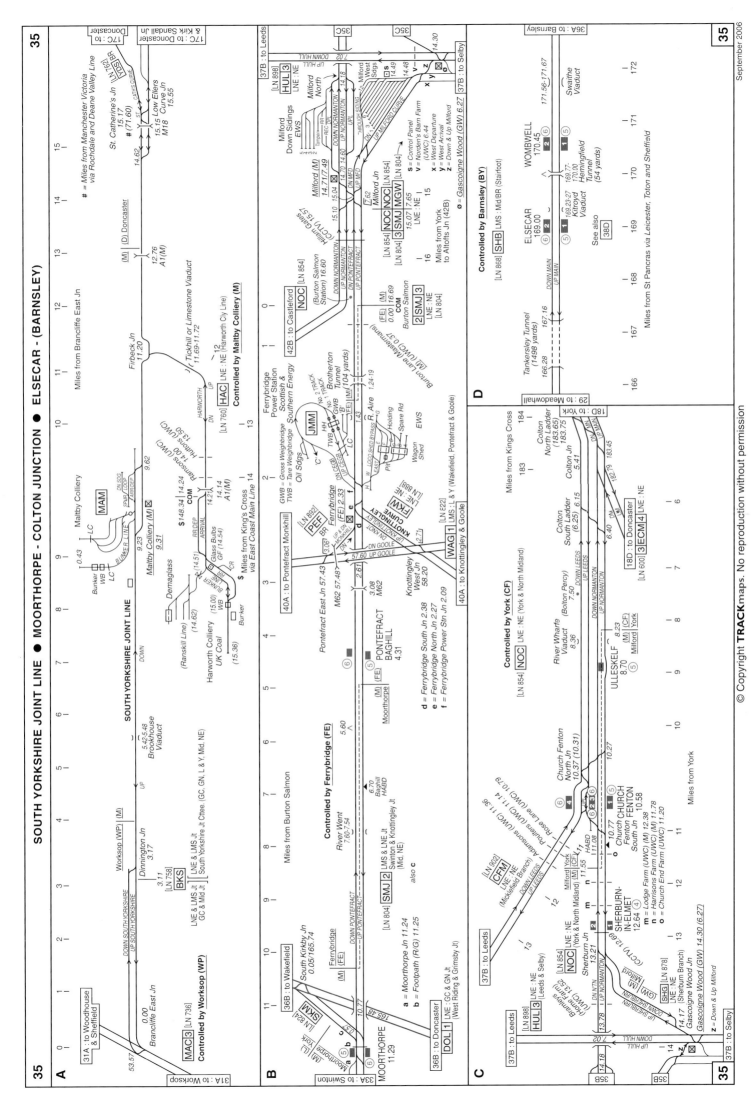

SOUTH YORKSHIRE JOINT LINE ● MOORTHORPE - COLTON JUNCTION ● ELSECAR - (BARNSLEY)

September 2006

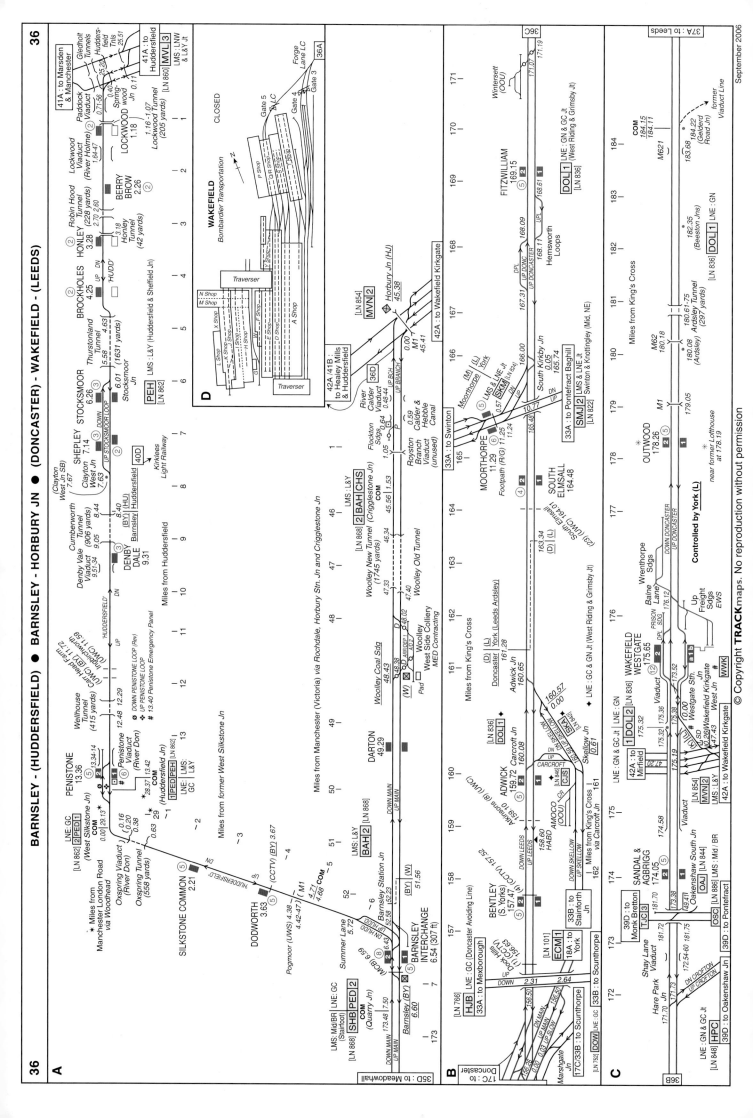

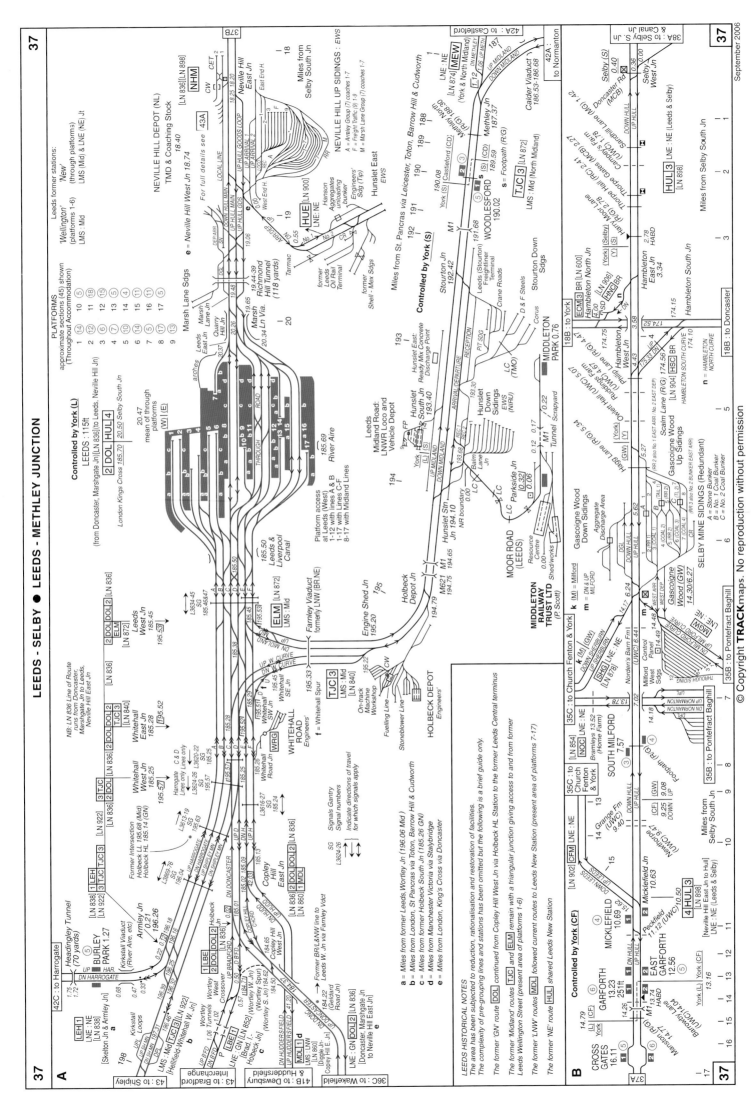

LEEDS - SELBY ● LEEDS - METHLEY JUNCTION

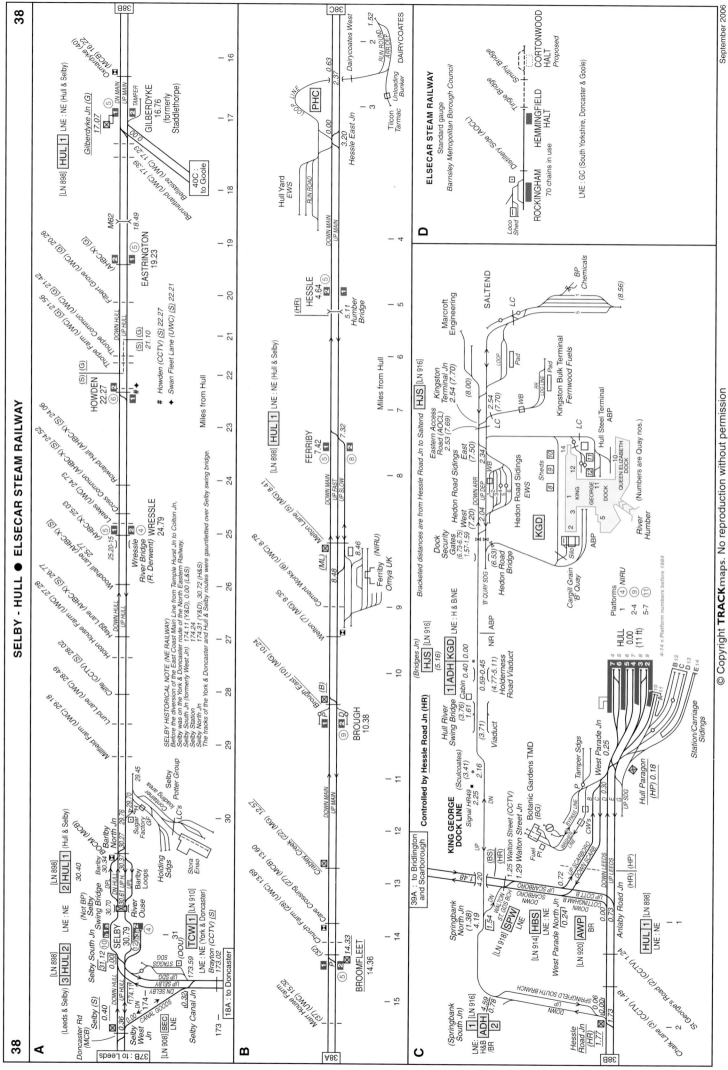

SELBY - HULL ● ELSECAR STEAM RAILWAY

September 2006

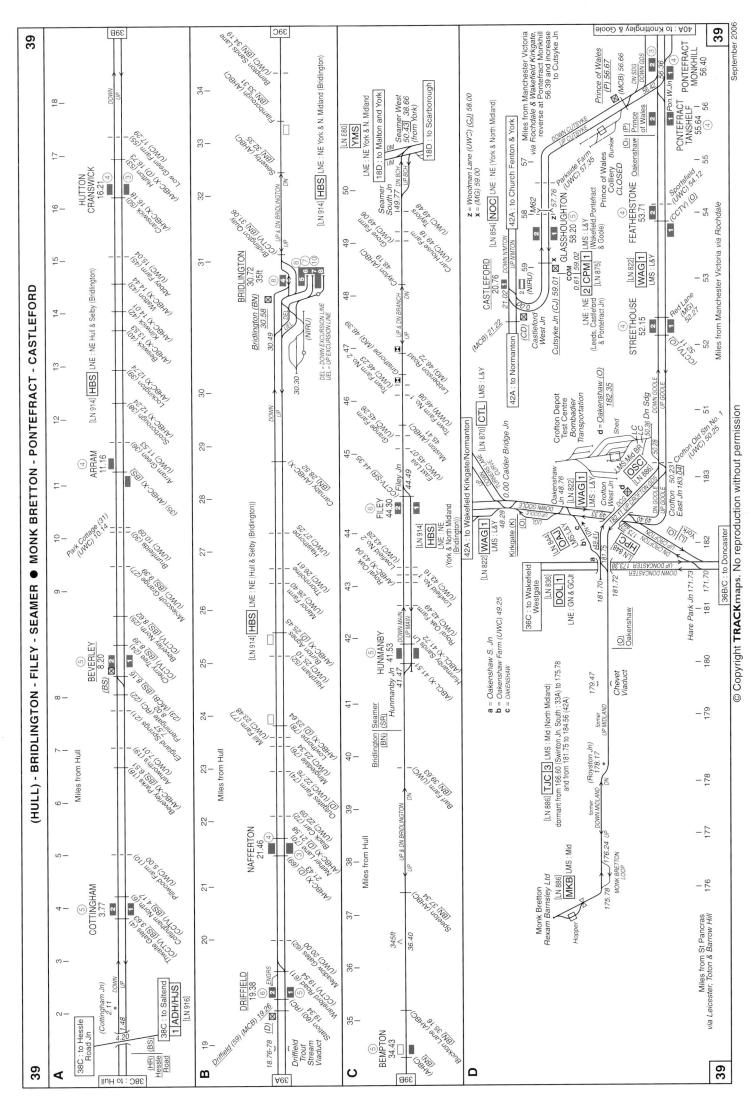

(HULL) - BRIDLINGTON - FILEY - SEAMER ● MONK BRETTON - PONTEFRACT - CASTLEFORD

September 2006

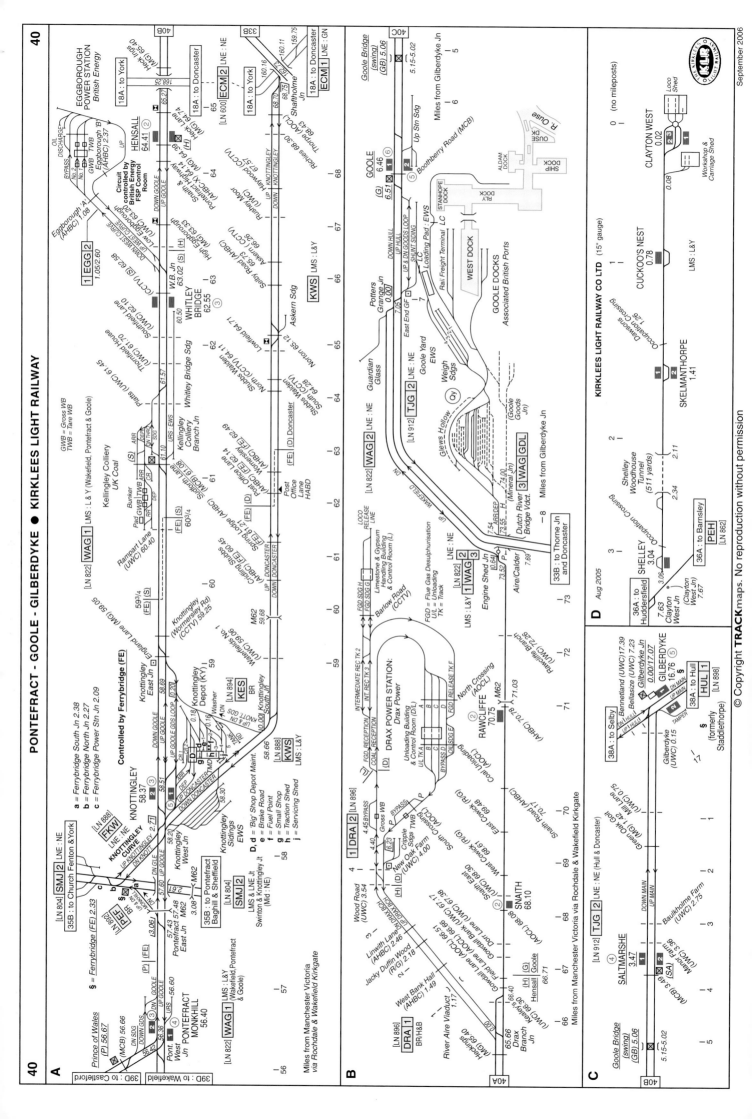

HEBDEN BRIDGE / MARSDEN - HUDDERSFIELD - MIRFIELD - (LEEDS) / HEALEY MILLS

A

z = River Calder Viaduct 31.16-31.20

Miles from Manchester Victoria via Rochdale

4 : 33B : to Todmorden and Manchester

Preston (PN) (HB)
LNW LNE
22.62 UP L&Y DN L&Y
23.12-17

Weasel Hall Viaduct (109 yards)

HEBDEN BRIDGE (HB) 23.50 / 23.55

DOWN MAIN / UP MAIN
URS

MYTHOLMROYD 24.68
Mytholmroyd Viaduct 24.60

[LN 854] MVN 2 LMS : L&Y (Manchester & Leeds)

Sowerby Tunnel (657 yards) 27.60

SOWERBY BRIDGE 28.51
Sowerby Viaduct 28.10 / 28.20

[LN 858] MRB LMS : L&Y (W. Riding Union)

Bank House Tunnel (214 yards) 30.57-30.67
R. Calder etc. (MR) 29.21 / 29.20
Milner Royd Jn

Copley Viaduct 31.36
Dryclough Jn 0.00
UP BCH 0.21-0.25
Salterhebble Down & Up Tunnels (91 yards)
R. Calder Viaduct 31.25-44

Halifax (H) / 43 : to Halifax

DOWN BRANCH 0.77
1.11
Greetland Jn (G) 30.77

Elland Tunnel (420 yards)
Elland (E) 31.61

River Calder Viaduct 29.73-30.12 / 29.76-30.00

'CALDER VALLEY LINE'

M62 35.36
Bradley Wood Jn 35.59

Heaby Mills (HM) (E)
BRIGHOUSE 34.31

[LN 854] MVN 2 LMS : L&Y (Manchester & Leeds) 31.16-31.20 0.67

[LN 860] MVL 4 LMS : LNW

* = Bradley Hall Farm No. 1 (UWC) (HM) 0.67
Ω = Heaton Lodge South Jn (28.78)
* = Heaton Lodge East Jn (Down) 37.49 (29.72)

River Calder
38.30 (30.54) 39.27
DOWN FAST 1 2 4 38.37
MIRFIELD 3
Mirfield Viaduct (River Calder)
41B 39.32 (31.56)

UP FAST / UP SLOW
DN HUDD
(29.25) 37.29 37.00 (29.54)
UP 29 0.301 0.24
Heaton Lodge Jn (up) 28.60
Ω Bradley Colne Viaduct
Bradley Jn 28.39
[LN 861] BBW LMS : L&Y
UP & DN BRADLEY BRANCH
DN HUDDERSFIELD 0.00 Bradley Tunnel (132 yards)
DEIGHTON 27.60
Healey Mills (HM) (HU)

[LN 860] 3 MVL 4 LMS : LNW 3

Huddersfield Viaduct 25.68 / 26.26

Platforms
1 (9) 5 (2)
2 (3) 6 (3)
4 (8) 10 8 (7)

Huddersfield Tunnels (696 yards)
HUDDERSFIELD 25.60
1 2 b 1 a LOOP
4 a 5 6 UP MAIN

Gledholt Tunnels
25.04 25.15 North 25.20
24.65 South 25.20
Springwood Jn 25.20 0.11 0.40
DN UP & DN HUDDERSFIELD SINGLE
(Gledholt Jn) 36A : to Barnsley

SLAITHWAITE 21.19
Golcar Viaduct 22.50
Milne Viaduct 23.50

21.34-45 Crimble Viaduct
21.00-07 Slaithwaite Viaduct

[LN 860] MVL 3 LMS : LNW
(Huddersfield & Manchester Railway & Canal)

Standedge Tunnel (3 miles, 66 yards)
Old tunnels { Down Slow / Up Slow }
650 ft

Diggle Jn (DE) (HU)
Huddersfield
LNW | LNE

MARSDEN 18.59
18.14 17.30
18.17 URS SLO
UPL 18.66 DRS

Miles from Manchester Victoria via Stalybridge

4 : 45C : to Stalybridge and Manchester

B

Miles from Manchester Victoria via Huddersfield

Batley Viaduct 34.60
Batley (Lady Anne) (MGW) 35.57

Jack Lane Viaduct 34.20
DEWSBURY 33.62 / 33.50
Dewsbury Railway St. EWS

Howley Park (UWC) 36.04
BATLEY 35.09
0.10
Lafarge

Thornhill LNW Jn 39.72
RAVENSTHORPE (32.28)
40.60 Thornhill Jn 32.16
'LNW' miles in brackets

(31.50)/(31.51) DN MAIN
39.32 39.27 UP L&Y
39.20 (31.44) UP FAST 39.26 DN MAIN
Mirfield East Jn

Morley Tunnel (1 mile, 1609 yards)
MORLEY 38.24
36.25
38.19
38.77
Churchwell Viaduct 39.40-44
M62 40.19
COTTINGLEY 40.02
(B) (L) 40.70

[LN 860] MDL 1 LMS : LNW (Leeds, Dewsbury & Manchester)

37A : to Leeds
(B) (L) York 40.70
41 (L) 36A

[LN 861] PEH LMS : L&Y

Healey Mills 'A' Jn 42.00
Healey Mills (Midland Jn) 0.00 41.62 42.06
Dewsbury East Jn 41.43
42.30

[LN 854] MVN 2 LMS : L&Y (Manchester & Leeds)
RUN ROUND LINE / UP L&Y DOWN L&Y

'C' Jn 42.70
Healey Mills (HM) 42.64
42.62 / 42.58 / 42.57

River Calder

Down Staging Sdgs (ex Staging Sdgs E)
Fuel Depot 43.00
Wagon Rep.
(Loco. Inspection & Fuelling Point) EWS

DS 1
DS 2
DS 3
HYM

LINE 'U' / LINE 'W'
LINE 'X' / LINE 'Y' / LINE 'Z'

EAST (DOWN) DEPARTURES 43.50
'B' DEP / 'A' DEP
West (Up) Departures

Down Primaries
Engineering Sidings (formerly Up Primary Sorting)

Up Staging Sdgs
Up Secondary Sorting Sdgs (16)
UP SOW

HEALEY MILLS YARD : EWS
Qy

43.10 / 43.31 Healey Mills 'B' Jn

'D' Jn 43.63
Horbury Station
HORBURY UGL 44.02
DOWN L&Y UP L&Y
Up Sidings
Storrs Hill Marcroft
44

42A : to Wakefield Kirkgate

41A / 41B

September 2006

TRACKmaps

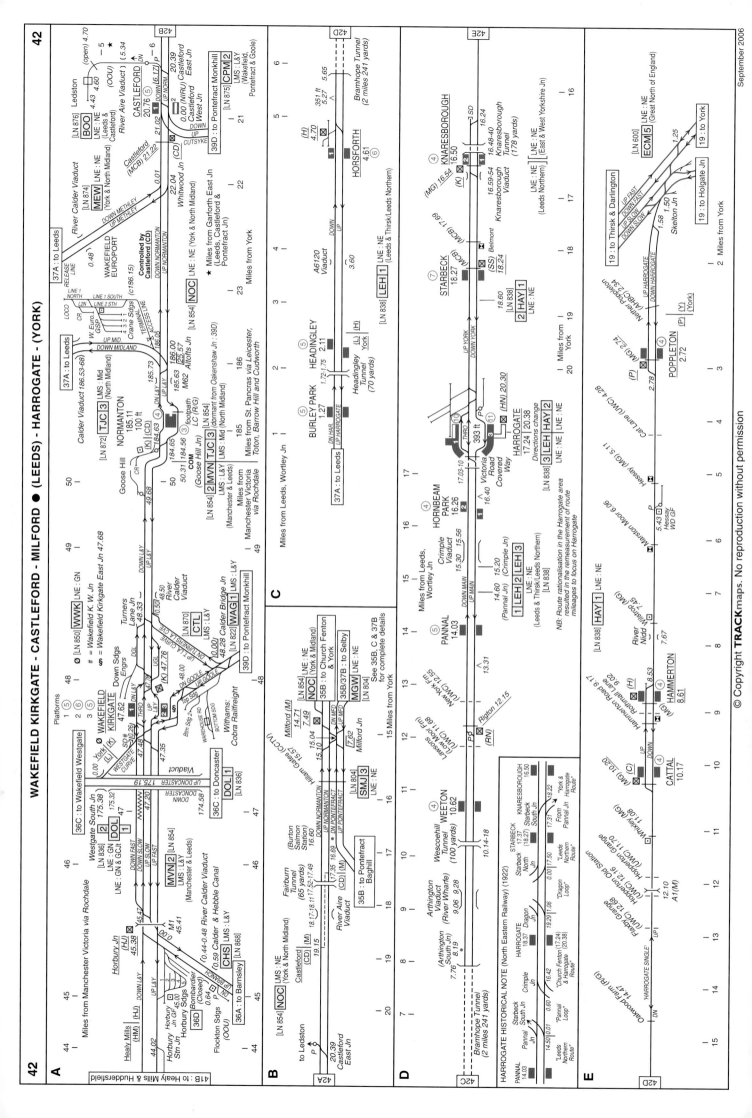

WAKEFIELD KIRKGATE - CASTLEFORD - MILFORD ● (LEEDS) - HARROGATE - (YORK)

September 2006

(LEEDS) - ILKLEY / KEIGHLEY / BRADFORD ● (LEEDS) - BRADFORD - HALIFAX

B

ABBEY LIGHT RAILWAY
KIRKSTALL ABBEY, LEEDS

BRIDGE ROAD 0.01

Sheds

KIRKSTALL ABBEY 0.22

Mill Race

LC 0.12

R. Aire

2ft gauge / 22ch

(Aug 2005)

37A : to Leeds

43

September 2006

205 Miles from St.Pancras via Cudworth

37A : to Leeds

Kirkstall Forge Viaduct (R. Aire) *99.09-04

UP SHIPLEY MAIN
DOWN SHIPLEY MAIN

LMS : Mid (Otley & Ilkley Extn)

ILK 1 [LN 924]

Springs Tunnel (77 yards) ~ 204

Greenbottom Tunnel (134 yards)

GUISELEY 205.22 444 ft

204.67
204.61
204.32 Esholt Jn
0.00

Esholt Trl (548 yds)
Esholt Viaduct 204.01
0.27
0.52
0.75-70

Apperley Lane Tunnel (75 yds)
HABD 201.40
UP 202
DN 202.03
202.64 202.61

APPERLEY

Apperley Jn 202.00
Calverley Vdct. (R. Aire) 201.27-17
Apperley Viaduct 203.43 203.10-02

[LN 922] TJC 3 LMS : Mid (Leeds & Bradford)

Thackley Tunnels (1518 yds)

MENSTON 206.53

ILK 1 [LN 924] LMS:Mid

(Burley Jn)

BURLEY-IN-WHARFEDALE 208.92

1.55
1.65
1.71
2.03
2.14

Baildon No. 2 Trl (274 yds)
Baildon No. 1 Trl (156 yds)
Tong Park Viaduct

Charlestown Viaduct (River Aire)

205.47 Shipley East Jn
UP SHIPLEY MAIN
DOWN SHIPLEY MAIN
205.54 Shipley East Jn
0.08/206.73
0.00/206.00 Shipley South Jn

Controlled by York (L)

Controlled by York (L)

LMS : LNE Jt : Mid & NE Jt (Otley & Ilkley)
UP ILKLEY MAIN
DOWN ILKLEY MAIN

BEN RHYDDING 210.21

Sun Lane (UWC) 208.50

BAILDON 2.29
BAILDON
3.00
3.06
2.41

[LN 926] GUE 2 LMS : Mid (Shipley & Guiseley)

SHIPLEY Platforms
1, 2, 3, 4, 5

Shipley 4, 5
205.72 Dockfield
206.00
206.09-6
206.25
205.51
Shipley Tunnel (55 yds)

FRIZINGHALL 206.67

SBF [LN 928] LMS : Mid (Leeds & Bradford)

ILKLEY 211.20 (318 ft)
211.08

Shipley W Jn 0.177
FORSTER SQ 0.00
WB RD
Crossley Evans scrapyard

BRADFORD FORSTER SQUARE 208.50 319 ft

ARR
DOWN FORSTER SQUARE MAIN
UP F SQ MAIN
ARR
208.08
208.26

BIB [LN 932]

COAL RDS

KEIGHLEY 212.06
211.74
River Worth Viaduct
SB (OOU)
0.12
0.16 River Worth

Keighley Stn Jn 212.00
Sdg GF
North GF
K & WVLR
West GF

54F : to Oxenhope (Worth Valley Rly)

BINGLEY 208.68
208.63-56 Bingley Tunnel (151 yds)

(Dowley Gap)
River Aire Viaduct 208.10

CROSSFLATTS 209.45

[LN 922] TJC 3 LMS : Mid (Leeds & Bradford Extn)

Miles from St.Pancras via Cudworth

Gorts (UWC) 213.15

44A : to Skipton

A

NEVILLE HILL DEPOT (NL)

Midland Main Line 18.40

(Leeds - see 37A)

NHM

Tyre Turning Lathe
Underframe Cleaning Shed
Train Maintenance Shed
Power Car Bays
Back Fitting Shop
DMU Repair Shed
Wall Sdgs
CW
Reception Sdgs
Train Servicing Shed
DMU Fuel Shed
Group 2 Carr. Sdgs
Departure Sdgs 1-9
Slip Road
PARKSIDE
DMU ARRIVAL
Waste Console
Dead Ends
Slip Road
PILOT LINE
LOCAL LINE
DOWN HULL MAIN
UP HULL MAIN

[LN 858] MRB LMS : L&Y (West Riding Union)

HUL 4

Bradford Interchange

Stabling Sdg

BRADFORD INTERCHANGE 40.27

40.03

Loco Road RR

[LN 852] MRB
LMS : L&Y [LN 858]

[LN 852] LMS: GN 3 LBE 2 2 LBE 1 LMS: GN

Laisterdyke Yard European Metal Recycling

[LN 852] 4 LBE 3 LMS: GN

COM

190.24 6.49 2 LBE 1 LMS: GN
(Laisterdyke East Jn)
190.50
190.43

(Hammerton Street Jn) 191.30
Hammerton Street Loop
(Laisterdyke West Jn)
191.18
191.42-36
Wakefield Rd. Trl. (132 yds)
191.68
191.78

Mill Lane Jn (St. Dunstans)

Miles from Kings Cross via former Birkenshaw Line
191

Bowling Jn

Miles from Manchester Victoria via Rochdale

Mill Lane Jn (M) 39.79
39.13 39.20
Bowling Tunnel (1648 yards)
38.18

New Furnace Tunnel (69 yds) 37.07-10 (Low Moor) 37.39

Wyke Tunnel (1365 yards)
36.12 36.74

Lightcliffe Tunnel (70 yds) 35.16-24
35.00 Bolton Hall Viaduct

Hipperholme Tunnel (388 yards) 34.05-22 34.67-70

Beacon Hill Tunnel (1105 yards) 33.10

[LN 858] MRB

HALIFAX 32.28

Beacon Hill Viaduct 32.26-36

Dryclough Junction 31.36

Reversing Sdg 388 ft (N) 32.40
(H) 32.02 (S)
DOWN MAIN
UP MAIN
DN
UP
0.00

HAL 1

[LN 888] HUL 4

41A : to Greetland Jn/Sowerby Bridge and Manchester

43

STANNINGLEY BYPASS 2.52

DOWN

BRAMLEY 3.15
3.68 (L)

(M) (L) York

NEW PUDSEY 4.77 4.74 4.40-32
Stanningley Viaduct
5.22
New Pudsey Tunnel (52 yds) 5.03-01
5.43
Stanningley Tunnel (455 yds)
5.68 5.69

Ducketts (R/G)

Miles from Holbeck West Jn

© Copyright **TRACK**maps. No reproduction without permission

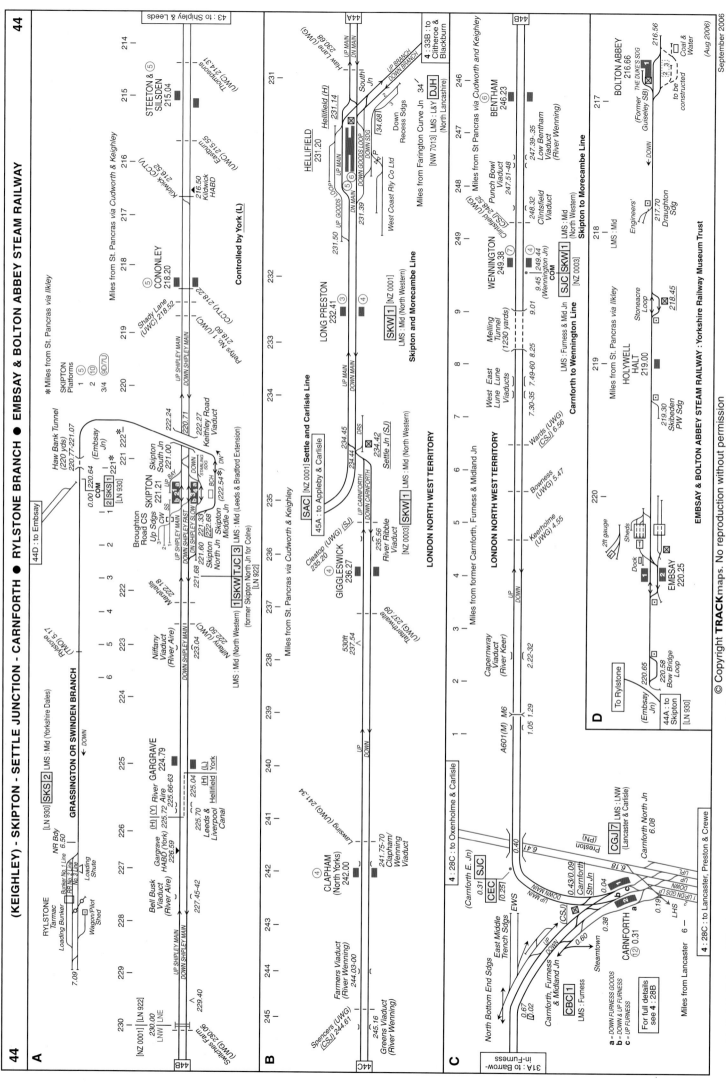

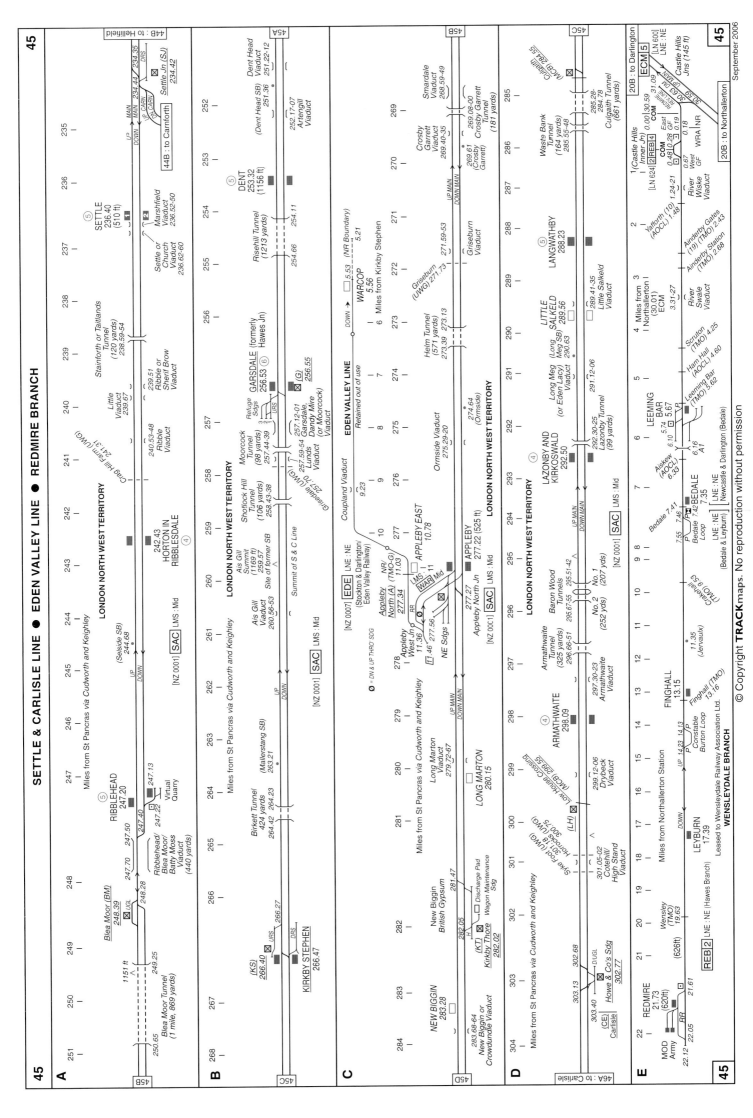

SETTLE & CARLISLE LINE ● EDEN VALLEY LINE ● REDMIRE BRANCH

September 2006

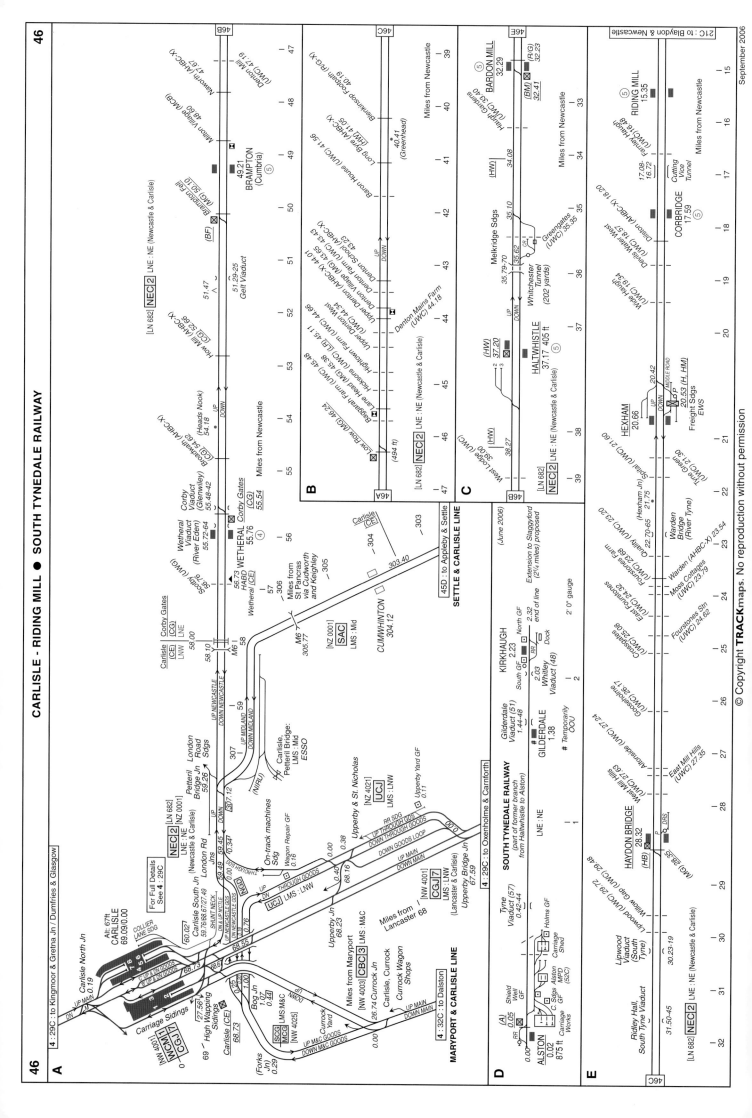

CARLISLE - RIDING MILL ● SOUTH TYNEDALE RAILWAY

46

© Copyright TRACKmaps. No reproduction without permission

September 2006

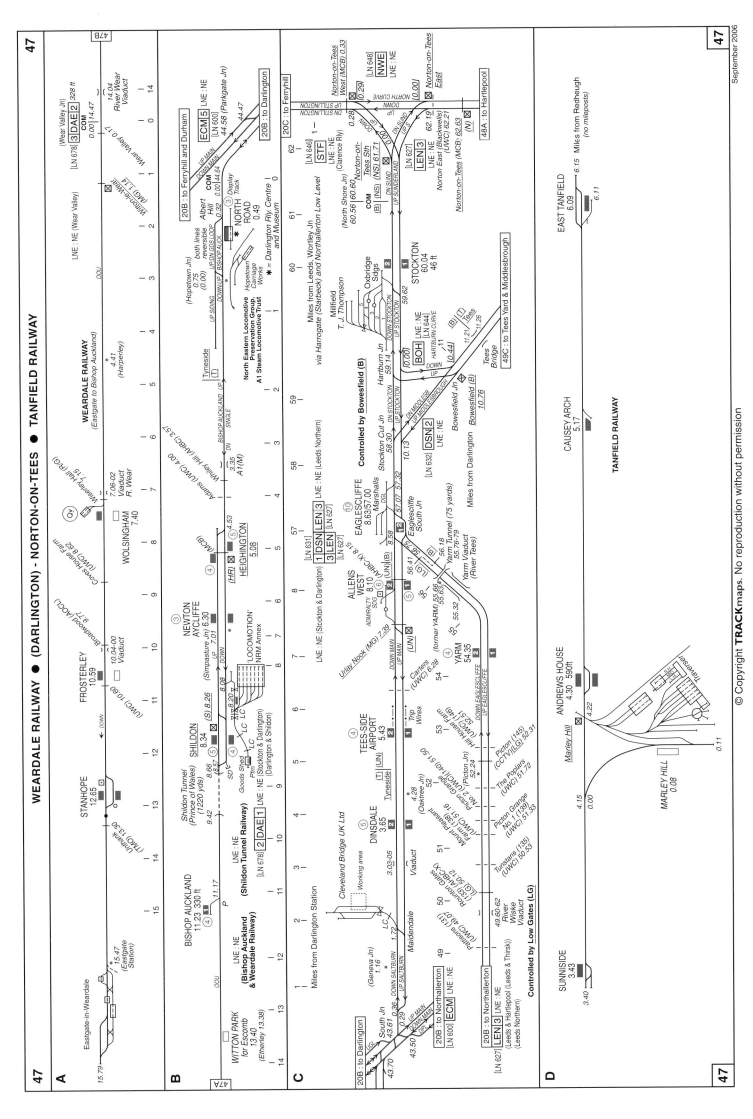

Section A

Hartlepool South Works
Corus

20 inch Mill

84 inch Pipe Mill

Crimdon Dene Viaduct

75.36-47

DOWN MAIN
UP SPUR

Cemetery North (CN) 73.49
LC
closed
Redland
Discharge Point

(NIRU)

[LN 627] LEN 3   LNE : NE (Leeds Northern)

Central Marine
(NIRU)
HLD   LNE : NE

Clarence Road (CR) 71.70

72.20
Hartlepool Docks (Linkflow)
Tees & Hartlepool Port Authority
Qy

Miles from Leeds, Wortley Jn via Harrogate (Starbeck) and Northallerton low level

[LN 627] LEN 3   LNE : NE (Stockton & Hartlepool) (Leeds Northern)

Church Street (CS) 71.40
4 7
Stranton HARTLEPOOL 71.55 17ft
71.22 (S)
71.14

Cliff House (CH) 70.08

Seaton Carew 69.36
[LN 627] LEN 3
DGL   DN MAIN
UP GOODS   EAST SDG
69.43 1 1
Cliff House South GF
New Ground Sdgs
Phillips Imperial Petroleum Refinery
SD   Ldg Gantry
North Tees (AOCL) 4.19
Seal Sands (AOCL) 4.7
UP GOODS

5.01
5.21
RR
0.00 Seal Sands Branch Jn
ICI Brinefield (open) 0.12
NEEB (open) 0.39
North/South Access (open) 0.71
DN   UP
BASF run-round loop
1.22
1.40
1.42 Rohm Hass (AOCL)
1.43 Monsanto Sdg Jn
1.46 Monsanto/BASF (AOCL)
Simon Storage South (Propylene)
1.52
2.11 SS Chemicals (AOCL)
2.16 Phillips No. 2 (AOCL)
2.22 Phillips No. 3 (AOCL)
2.23
BASF
Monsanto (AOCL) 1.46
Simon Storage North
Seal Sands Storage 0.06
Seal Sands Road (AOCL) 0.05
Seal Sands run-round loop
2.42
2.44
SES   LNE : NE

Hartlepool Power Stn British Energy:
Nuclear Electric Division
Unloading / Loading Bay
LS
West ILC (open) 1.51

GANTRY LINE
Greatham (GM) 67.8
(GM) (MOB)
(GM)
67.52
67.6
DOWN (Haverton Hill)   UP
West ILC (open) 1.02
Seaton Snook
Graythorpe 0.00 Seaton Snook Jn
[LN 656] SOT   LNE : NE
(AOCL) 0.25
Port Clarence Jn 3.05
(Port Clarence)
Phillips Loop
Phillips Sdg 3.25
3.08
[LN 652] 1 POC 2
Port Clarence: Enron (open) 0.52
Bells Bank EWS
Ferndale Sdg
Pad
Marcroft
HAH 2
Haverton Hill South (AOCL) 1.9
ICI Petro-Chemical Division
(Billingham Wharf)
Billingham Reach
Billingham Back Branch
Marcroft
Marcroft
ICI Departures
Portrack Sidings
Qy

Miles from Leeds, Wortley Jn via Ripon
63.64

Greatham Viaduct 66.41-43
Cowpen Lane (AHBC)(X) 65.44
Seaton-on-Tees 1.51
Belasis Lane 1.04
1.13
1.08 0.00
Haverton Hill (Haverton Hill) 2.02   DOWN
HAH
Haverton Hill Exchange Sidings
ICI Chemicals & Polymer Gp.
Qy
Haverton Hill : East Grid

Billingham Jn 63.69
BILLINGHAM 64.47 7
2 1
[LN 652] POC 1   LNE : NE (Clarence Rly)
[LN 627] LEN 3
DOWN UP
0.00

Norton-on-Tees 62.62
(N) (B)
Billingham (Mc) 63.60

47C : to Stockton/Ferryhill

76 75 74 73 72 71 70 69 68 67 66 65 64 63

Section B

B

NETWORK RAIL (Metro trains only)

$ = Combined Bi-directional 3/4 in separate designated platforms
# = Queen Alexandra Bridge River Wear Vdct 89.77-90.11
⊘ = Monkwearmouth Jn

Controlled from Tyneside (T)

49A : to Newcastle

SEABURN 91.32 3
STADIUM OF LIGHT 90.48 3
ST PETERS 90.08 3
[LN 627] LEN 3   LNE : NE (Brandling Jn)

Swing Bridge
2.44
Petrofina
LC
2.08

Sunderland South Dock
i/c Port of Sunderland Authority & European Metal Recycling

6 SOUTH HYLTON 3.17
1 3.20
2 3.11

[LN 628] NEK

PALLION 1.67 3
DN S.HYLTON
UP S.HYLTON
MILLFIELD 1.01 3
UNIVERSITY 0.44 3
[LN 662] HNB

PARK LANE 0.21
SUNDERLAND 0.00 89.60
9 89.60
$ 3 1
2 4 89.64
Sunderland North End 89.71
89.64 92ft
Sunderland North Tunnel (256 yds)
0.17 0.00
89.49 89.51
89.56
Sunderland South End Jn
89.38 89.39 45
Umbrella 89.49
Sunderland South Tunnels
NR | PSA
1.53

Tyneside (T)
DN MAIN
UP MAIN
88.60
89.06 711 yds 127 yds
DN SUN
UP SUN

No. 18
No. 19
No. 5 SDG   RR
ARRIVAL
Londonderry Sdgs

former Murton/Hawthorn Washery Branch
Ryhope Grange (RG) 87.63
Ryhope Grange Sdgs
OOU No. 1
RR No. 3
Grangetown (open) 0.30
87.47 0.00
[LN 662] HNB (Londonderry) HENDON BRANCH (NIRU)
Davidsons North 87.20
Davidsons South (UWC) 86.57
Hall Dene (MC&B) 85.24

[HD]

[LN 627] LEN 3   LNE : NE (Londonderry)

Polka Sdg
Dawdon (DN) 84.22
SEAHAM 84.49
84.44 1
84.11
Dawdon Dene Viaduct 83.31-37
1.65
Dawdon 1.36
NR/Port of Seaham
UP
Pad
Under Track Unloading
Cargo Durham Warehouse
Seaham Harbour EWS and Lafarge
[SEA] LNE : NE

Hawthorn Dene Viaduct 81.67-72
[LN 627] LEN 3   LNE : NE (Leeds Northern)

Castle Eden Viaduct 78.15-26
(Easington) 80.33 180 ft
(Horden) 78.44
Blackhills Farm (UWC) 78.78

Miles from Leeds, Wortley Jn via Harrogate (Starbeck) and Northallerton low level

(Blackhall) 76.89
Blackhall Rocks 76.76

48A

92 91 90 89 88 87 86 85 84 83 82 81 80 79 78 77

September 2006

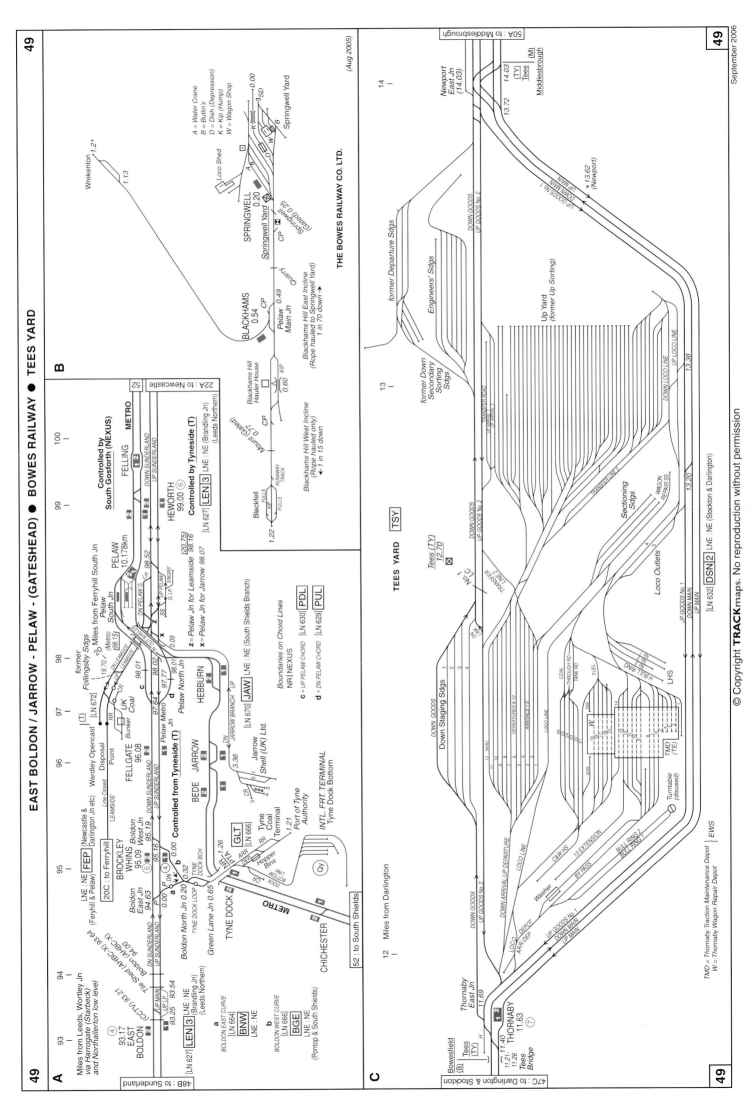

MIDDLESBROUGH - REDCAR / NUNTHORPE

A

Buried
Raw Ore Stocks
Conveyor
Loading Pad (OOU)
Limestone
Coal

REDCAR ORE TERMINAL
Corus
Blended Ore Stocks

REDCAR MINERAL TERMINAL
Corus

Raw Coal Stocks
Blended Coal Stocks

Bunkers
Wagon Loading Control Room
Bunkers

Loading Bank
WB's
LC
Iron Plating
Area

REDCAR BLAST FURNACE

Redcar
Corus
REDCAR WORKS (Qy)

SB
CR
(Qy)

2 [LN 632] DSN 3
COM 21.72 22.16
LNE : NE (Stockton & Darlington/ Middlesbrough & Redcar)

51A : to Saltburn

Cleveland Potash
1 & 2 = Potash
1 = Loco line
3 = Loaded
5 = Empties

TEES DOCK
Tees & Hartlepool Port Authority

Tees Bulk Handling
Steel Export Terminal

LC

ARRIVAL IN (OOU)
DEPARTURE OUT (OOU)
ORE DEP
ORE ARR
Tod Point Jn 20.50
20.13 20.50

Redcar Ore Terminal Jn 20.05
20 [LN 638] WCI
20.10 20.21
0.48

NR Huntsman Chemicals
1.03

1 2 BRITISH STEEL REDCAR (3) 20.56

HOT METAL RAILWAY

Shell Jn 0.00 19.32
Former Shell Branch 0.31
WILTON BRANCH

DOWN MAIN
UP MAIN

Lackenby No.4 Grid
Lackenby No.3 Grid
SB SB SB

Control Tower
Heavy Engineering Spares Store

ICI Wilton Jn 0.00/1.38
East Gate Mount (open) 1.34
Boundary Road North (open)
Northway (open)
Eastway (open)
Diluent Spur
LC

Repair Shop
SIDINGS
Loco Shed
STEELWORKS

COAL LINE
DEPARTURE
ARRIVAL
Outwards Sdgs
Inwards Sdgs
INWARD
OUTWARD
[LN 640]
Transit Shed
LS

Huntsman Chemicals
Chlorine handling plant
No. 5 Depot

Coal Hopper
North Gate (open) 2.24
Coal Access 2.07
CR P
CR
Marcroft
0.70

T&HPA
NR
Grangetown (G) Grangetown Jn
19 [LN 636]
CORUS LINE
18.76
18.65 18.51 18.41
18.34
Slag Rd (TMO) 18.67
(Qy)
DN
No.2 Grid GF
CORUS
NR
Lackenby No.2 Grid

GRANGETOWN
Grangetown 18.41
BEAM MILL LINE

Beam Mill Jn 18.03

DOWN GOODS
UP GOODS
DOWN MAIN
UP MAIN

18 Miles from Darlington

South Bank Jn 17.31
SOUTH BANK (4) 17.40

[LN 632] DSN 2
LNE : NE (Stockton & Darlington)

Steel Services Stocking Ground
Steel Services

Export Bay
Coil Plate Mill
Universal Beam Mill
LACKENBY
No. 2 Primary Mill
Corus

BOS Plant
Concast Plant
Torpedo & Ladle Repair Shop

Corus Constructional and Industrial Teeside Cast Products
Lackenby Works
Middlesbrough

Cleveland (Wilton) Freightliner Terminal
Freightliner Terminal LC (Gated)
HMD Filling Bay
2.61

Fuel Pt
LC LC LC

Morton Grange Farm No.4 (UWC) 5.50
Morton Carr (AOCL) 4.68
(Nunthorpe Jn) 5.30

LC

© Copyright TRACKmaps. No reproduction without permission

September 2006

B

z = Under Track Unloading Facility

Warehouse
Ayrton Terminal
A. V. Dawson
Dent's Wharf
A. V. Dawson
Forty Foot Rd LC
Depot Road LC

Castle Cement Co. Depot (OOU)
Marcroft
WB
z
INLET
OUTLET
MARSH BRANCH
Ayrton Sdgs
FIRST SHUNT LINE
SALT RD
Pad

Middlesbrough Goods Yard
EWS
Cobra Railfreight

Newport East Jn 14.03
13.73

14.65
[LN 632] DSN 2
(T) (M) Tees 14.03
LNE : NE (Stockton & Darlington)

49C : to Tees Yard & Thornaby

DOWN GOODS
DOWN MAIN
UP MAIN
UP GOODS
14.60
14.65
WEST END DK
(M) 14.71

a 2 b
a 1 b
(M) 14.71
50B
MIDDLESBROUGH 15.00 (10)

15
14
17
16

North Sdgs
Stockton Haulage (NIRU)
Tees Works Sdg
16.06
16.37 (Inner Jn) Eston Branch)
former BS Coke Ovens Line
OOU
DOWN
UP
15.76
(16.06)
CARGO FLEET
Whitehouse

Engrs
Carriage Sdgs

MIDDLESBROUGH 15.00
28 ft

15.18
15.23
0.00
DOWN GOODS
UP GOODS
DOWN MAIN
UP MAIN
Guisborough

a 2 b
a 1 b
(M) 14.71
(1) (M) Tees

14.65

[LN 632] DSN 2
LNE : NE (Stockton & Darlington/ Middlesbrough & Guisborough) and Ayrton Branch

UP NUNTHORPE SINGLE
DN
= Cargo Fleet Rd (CCTV) (M) 0.14
Controlled by Middlesbrough (M)

MARTON (formerly ORMESBY) (4) 2.56

GYPSY LANE (4) 3.60
Marton Lane (ABCL) 3.62

NUNTHORPE (4)
4.25 287 ft
Marton Lane (ABCL) 3.62
UP LOOP
UP & DN LOOP
(N)
(MCB) 4.27
4.31
4.12

[LN 634] MBW 1
LNE : NE (Stockton & Darlington/ Middlesbrough & Guisborough) and Ayrton Branch

Nunthorpe to Whitby No Signalman Token with Remote Token Stations (RTS)
Nunthorpe to Whitby No Signalman Token

51B : to Whitby

— 1 — 2 — 3 — 4 — 5 — 6

REDCAR - SALTBURN - CARLIN HOW ● WHITBY BRANCH ● NORTH YORKSHIRE MOORS RAILWAY

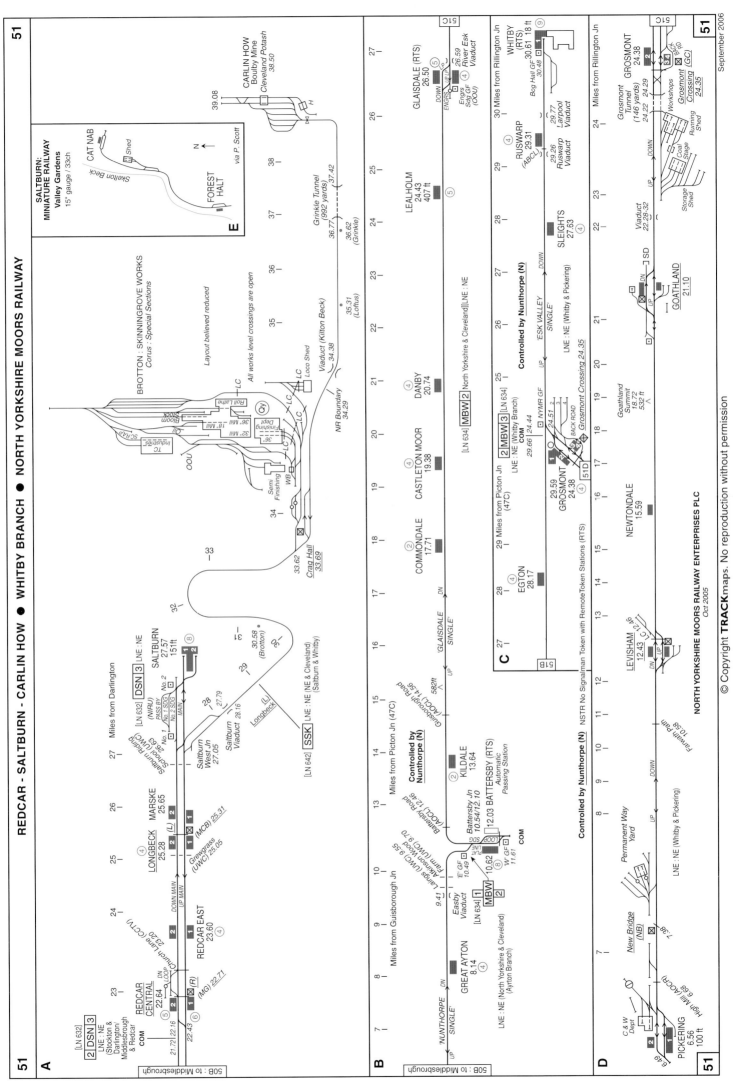

E SALTBURN: MINIATURE RAILWAY
Valley Gardens
15" gauge / 33ch

September 2006

TYNE & WEAR PASSENGER TRANSPORT EXECUTIVE METRO (NEXUS)

M **X**

A All distances on this page are metric;
station distances are from point of origin,
28 metres north of Gosforth South Junction.

Electrification at 1500V dc

This map is a full-page schematic diagram of the Tyne & Wear Metro network showing stations, junctions, distances and track layouts.

September 2006

Stations and features shown include:

WHITLEY BAY 11.959, MONKSEATON 10.918, CULLERCOATS 12.698, SDG LOOP, WEST MONKSEATON 9.657, Footpath (Murton), SHIREMOOR 7.721, NORTHUMBERLAND PARK 6.660, Stephenson Railway Museum, MUSEUM, NORTH TYNESIDE STEAM RAILWAY 1mile 62chains, PALMERSVILLE 4.928, Benton (North) 0.05, Benton Jn 4.24/0.00, NETWORK RAIL, 22B : to Morpeth, 23C : to Bedlington, OUT LOOP, IN LOOP, Footpath 5.552, Benton Reversing Sidings, BENTON 2.869, Benton East GF, Benton Station Jns 3.054, 22B : to Newcastle, FOUR LANE ENDS 2.092, LONGBENTON 1.223, Gosforth East Jn 0.610, SOUTH GOSFORTH 0.249, Stoneyhurst Road, ILFORD ROAD 0.790, Point of origin : 0 km, WEST JESMOND 1.550, Jesmond Jn 2.586, former JESMOND BR Station 2.898, AVOIDING LINE, Gosforth Depot (see inset), Gosforth Middle Jn, Gosforth South Jn, Control Centre, Christon Rd, REGENT CENTRE 1.186, Gosforth West Jn 1.046, KENTON, WANSBECK ROAD 2.125, FAWDON 2.660, Brunton Lane (AOCL), KINGSTON PARK 4.091, BANK FOOT 4.842, Station Road (AOCL), CALLERTON PARKWAY 7.157, Callerton Lane (AOCL), Woolsington Bridleway, AIRPORT 8.162, 8.228, continued above, continued below, TYNEMOUTH 14.631, NORTH SHIELDS 16.459 (Bay 16.552), North Shields Tunnel, Preston Refuge Siding (aka Bagnall's Siding), MEADOW WELL 17.792, Hylton Street Permanent Way Depot, PERCY MAIN 18.396, HOWDON 19.708, Howdon Viaduct, HADRIAN ROAD 21.157, Limekiln Road HGV Crossing, WALLSEND 22.276, WALKERGATE 24.058, CHILLINGHAM ROAD 24.896, Shields Rd Tunnel, Byker Tunnel, BYKER 26.011, Byker Viaduct (815m), Ouse Burn, Stoddart Street Sdgs, MANORS 27.648, MANORS SPUR, SHIELDS (1235m), HAYMARKET 3.548, Prudhoe St, JESMOND 2.760, ST JAMES 28.731, 28.772, MONUMENT 4.060/28.290, CENTRAL STATION 4.577, Forth Banks Tunnel Mouth, Queen Elizabeth II Bridge (352m), Tyne, River, Greensfield Tunnel Mouth, GATESHEAD 5.937, GATESHEAD STADIUM 7.093, FELLING 8.245, HEWORTH 9.283, PELAW 10.178, Bill Quay 11.243, Pelaw North Jn, Pelaw South Jn, Pelaw Sidings, Reyrolles 12.182, South Drive Crossing, HEBBURN 13.376, JARROW 15.400, BEDE 17.300, TYNE DOCK 19.297, Tyne Dock Tunnel 170m, CHICHESTER 20.653, SOUTH SHIELDS 21.972, Emergency Over-run, Crossgate Viaduct 233m, NR 97.77 Pelaw Metro, NR 98.01, NR 97.64, Pelaw Flyover 33.5m, 49A : to Sunderland, 49A : to Wardley; Leamside Line, 49A : to Newcastle, a = DOWN PELAW CHORD, z = UP PELAW CHORD, 18.060 Approx Proposed New Station

GOSFORTH DEPOT
Cheswick Drive Crossing, AVOIDING LINE (1235m), Depot Panel, Top Shed, CW, Oil Neck, West Rec, Headshunt, Gosforth West Jn 1.046, Gosforth Middle Jn, Christon Rd, Gosforth East Jn 0.610, EAST DEP, EAST REC, To Gosforth South Jn

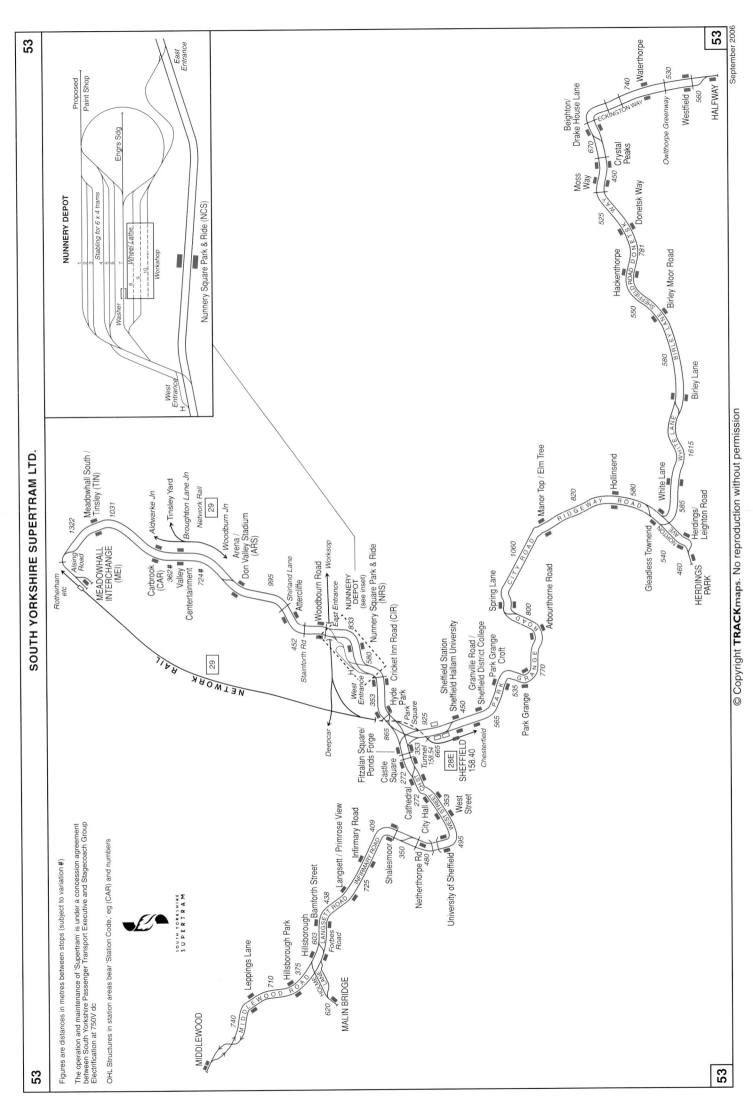

SOUTH YORKSHIRE SUPERTRAM LTD.

Figures are distances in metres between stops (subject to variation #)

The operation and maintenance of 'Supertram' is under a concession agreement between South Yorkshire Passenger Transport Executive and Stagecoach Group
Electrification at 750V dc

OHL Structures in station areas bear 'Station Code', eg (CAR) and numbers

NUNNERY DEPOT

Proposed
Paint Shop

East
Entrance

Engrs Sdg

1
2
3
4 *Stabling for 6 x 4 trams*
5
6
7

Wheel Lathe

8
9
10

Washer

Workshop

West
Entrance

Nunnery Square Park & Ride (NCS)

© Copyright TRACKmaps. No reproduction without permission

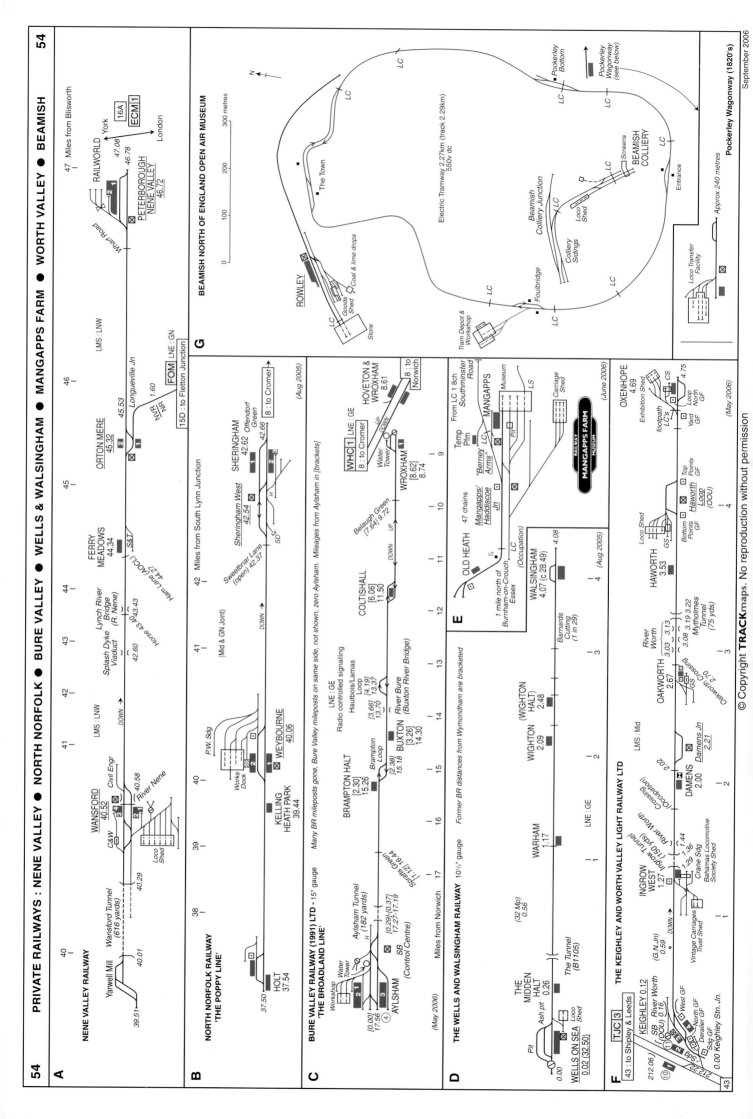

Index

In creation of this index, the full listing of locations and assets was subjected to a mild cull, made to arbitrary rules. The vast majority remain, including earlier locations of now-defunct assets (given in brackets) and most level crossings, to assist the reader in searching the Maps. Generally, private and preserved railways are limited to the main title (in *italics*) with individual locations omitted.

Location	Ref
CHESTERFIELD	28E
CHESTER-LE-STREET	21A
Chesterton Jn Sidings	11C
Chettisham LC (AHBC-X)	13C
Chevet Viaduct	39D
Chevington LC & North Crossovers	23A
CHICHESTER (Metro)	49A, 52
CHILLINGHAM ROAD (Metro)	22A, 52
Chillingham Road Jn	22A
CHINGFORD	10B
Chippenham Jn	12D
Chitts Hill LC (Gatebox)	5E
Chivers LC (AHBC-X)	13A
Choppington LC (AHBC)	23C
Chord Jn	2B
Christian Street Jn	3A
Christon Bank LC (CCTV)	23A
Church Dam LC	8
Church End Farm LC	35C
Church Farm LC	38B
CHURCH FENTON	35C
Church House Farm LC	5E
Church Lane (Newark) LC (CCTV)	16C
Church Lane (Norfolk) LC (TMO)	13B
Church Lane (Redcar) LC (CCTV)	51A
Church Lane Crossovers & LC	5C
Church Lane LC (Spalding)	26D
Church Lane LC (Brundall)	8
Church Lane LC (Reedham)	8
Church Street (Hartlepool) LC (CCTV)	48A
Church Street LC (AHBC-X) (Ingatestone)	5C
Church Viaduct	45A
Churchfield Road LC (CCTV)	1A
Churwell Viaduct	41B
CLACTON	6A
Clacton SB (C)	6A
CLAPHAM (North Yorks)	44B
Clapham Viaduct	44B
CLAPTON	10B
Clapton Jn	1B, 10B
Clara Vale LC (AHBC-X)	21C
Clarborough Jn & Tunnel	31B
Clarence Road (Hartlepool) SB (CR)	48A
Clarence Yard Jn	14A
Clark and Butchers LC	12C
Clarks LC	20B
Claxby & Usselby LC (AHBC-X)	28A
Claxby Gatehouse LC (AHBC-X)	28A
Claydon LC (CCTV)	6C
Claypole LC (CCTV)	16C
Clayton West Jn	36A
Clayton West Jn SB (former)	36A, 40D
Clayway LC	12A
Cleatop LC	44B
CLEETHORPES	32A
CLEETHORPES COAST LIGHT RAILWAY	28D
Clements No. 1 LC	27E
Cleveland (Wilton)	50B
Cleveland Bridge UK Ltd	47C
Cliff Quay	6B
Cliffe House SB (CH)	48A
Cliffe LC (CCTV)	38A
Cliffords Farm LC	10A
Clifton LC (CCTV)	22B
(Clifton SB)	19
Clintsfield LC	44C
Clintsfield Viaduct	44C
Clipstone Colliery (former)	30A
Clipstone SB (SJ) & Jns	30A
Clowne Single line	30A
Coakesworth Farm No. 2 LC	23C
Coal Access LC	50B
Coal Import & Export Terminals (Immingham)	32B
Coal Road LC	4B
Coal Unloading (Drax) LC (AOCL)	40B
Cockspin Road LC (AHBC-X)	12C
Coffue Drove LC	13C
COLCHESTER (NORTH)	6A
COLCHESTER TOWN (formerly ST. BOTOLPHS')	6A
(Coldham Lane Jn)	11C
Coldham LC (TMO)	13C
Coles Harbour LC	12A
COLLINGHAM	27E
Colne Jn	6A
COLNE VALLEY RAILWAY Co Ltd	4D
Colne Viaduct	41A
Coltishall Lane LC	8
Colton Ladders & Jns	18B, 35C
Colwick LC (CCTV)	25A
Colwick North Jn	25A
Commercial Road LC	8A
Common Road LC	18C
COMMONDALE	51B
Concrete Road LC	12A
CONISBROUGH	33A
Connington	15D
CONONLEY	44A
Cononly LC (CCTV)	44A
Coopers Lane Jn	11B
Coopies Lane LC (AHBC)	22B
Copenhagen Jn	1A, 14A
Copenhagen Tunnels	14A
Copley Hill Jns	37A
Copley Viaduct	41A
Copmanthorpe No. 2 LC (R/G)	18B
Copperas LC	9B
Coppermill North Jn	1B, 10A
CORBRIDGE	46E
Corby Gates SB (CG) & LC	46A
(Corby Glen)	16B
Corby Viaduct	46A
Cornard LC (ABCL)	5E
Coryton BP Refinery	4B
Cotehill (High Stand) Viaduct	45D
Cotgrave Colliery West Jn	25A
Cottage Lane LC (AHBC)	27E
Cottam Power Station	31B
COTTINGHAM	39A
COTTINGLEY	41B
Country End Jn	10A
(County School)	13B
Coupland Viaduct	45C
Couplands LC	26B
Cousins LC	18D
Cousins No 2 LC	5D
Covered Way (Junction Rd)	1A
Cow Green Emergency Crossover	6C
Cowpen Lane LC (AHBC-X)	48A
(Cowton)	20A, 20B
Coxhoe	20C
Cox's Walk LC	25B
Crabley Creek SB & LC (MG)	38B
Cradburns No. 4 LC	25B
Crag Hall SB	51A
Crag Hill Farm LC	45A
Crag Mill LC (CCTV)	23B
Crakehall LC (TMO)	45E
Crambeck LC	18C
CRAMLINGTON	22B
Cranbourne LC (R/G-X)	11A
Crankley Point LC (R/G)	27D
Cranswick LC (AHBC-X)	39A
Creaksea Place No. 1 LC	10A
Creasey's (Rye Meads) LC	11A
Crescent Jn, Shops & Sidings	16A
CRESSING	5D
Cresswell GF	30A
CRESWELL	30A
CREWS HILL	24A
Creykes LC (R/G)	33B
CRICKLEWOOD	1A
Cridling Stubbs LC (AHBC)	40A
Crigglestone Jn	36A
Crimble Viaduct	41A
Crimdon Dene Viaduct	48A
Crimple Jn	42D
Crimple Viaduct	42D
Croft Jn & Viaduct	20B
Crofton Depot & Jns	39D
Crofton Old Station LC	39D
CROMER	8
Cromwell Lane LC (CCTV)	16C
Cromwell Road LC (ABCL)	8
Crosby Garrett Viaduct and Tunnel	45C
(Crosby Garrett)	45C
(Crosby Mines)	34A, 34B
Cross Common LC (AHBC-X)	38A
CROSS GATES	37A
Cross Lane LC (AHBC)	27E
CROSSFLATS	43
Crossgates LC	46E
CROUCH HILL	1B
Crouch Valley Line	10A
(Crow Park)	17A
Crowdundle Viaduct	45C
CROWLE	33B
Crown Hill Tunnel	1B
Crown Point Depot & Control Tower (CP)	7A
Croxdale Viaduct	20C
Croxton LC (AHBC-X)	13A
CUFFLEY	24A
Culgaith LC, SB & Tunnel	45D
CULLERCOATES (Metro)	52
Cumberworth Tunnel	36A
Cumwhinton	46A
Currock Jn	46A
CUSTOM HOUSE	2C
Cut Throat Lane LC (R/G)	5D
Cutsyke Jn SB (CJ) & LC (MG)	39D
Cutting Vice Tunnel	46E
DAGENHAM DOCK	4A
DAGENHAM EAST (LUL)	3B
DAGENHAM HEATHWAY (LUL)	3B
Daines/Mayhew LC	6C
Dairycoates	38B
Dairycoates West LC	38B
DALSTON KINGSLAND	1B
Dalston Western Junction SB (DL)	1B
Dam Dykes LC (CCTV)	22B
Damgate LC	8
DANBY	51B
(Danby Wiske)	20B
DARLINGTON	20B
DARLINGTON RAILWAY CENTRE & MUSEUM	47B
DARNALL	29
DARSHAM	8
Darsham LC (AHBC)	8
DARTON	36A
Davidsons North & South LCs	48B
Daw Lane LC (CCTV)	18A
Dawden Dene Viaduct	48B
Dawdon Jn & SB (DN)	48B
Dawdys LC (ACOL)	8
Dawes Lane Jn & LC (AOCL)	34A
Dean Street Crossover	22A
(Dearne Jn)	33A
Decoy Farm LC	9A
Decoy Sidings, North and South Jns	17C
Deep Wharf LC	4A
Deepcar	29
DEIGHTON	41A
Demaglass	35A
Denaby LC (CCTV)	33A
DENBY DALE	36A
DENT	45B
(Dent Head SB)	45B
Dent Head Viaduct	45B
Denton Farm & Mains Farm LCs	46B
Denton Mill LC	46A
Denton School & Village LCs	46B
Dent's Wharf	50A
(Denver Jn)	12A
Denver LC (AHBC)	12A
DERBY ROAD	9A
DEREHAM	13B
Dereham Central SB	13B
Dernford LC (R/G)	11C
DERWENT VALLEY LIGHT RAILWAY	19A
Devils Water West LC	46E
DEVONS ROAD (DLR)	3A
Devonshire Street	2B
DEWSBURY	41B
Digswell Jn & (Welwyn) Viaduct	15A, 15B
Dilston LC(AHBC-X)	46E
Dimmocks Cote LC (AHBC-X)	11C
Dinnington Jn	35A
DINSDALE	47C
DISS	6C
Dock Hills LC (CCTV)	17C, 36B
Dock Junction North	1A
Dock Lane LC	9A
Dockfield Jn	43
Doddington Road LC (CCTV)	27E
DODWORTH	36A
Dodworth LC (CCTV)	36A
DONCASTER	17C
Doncaster Road LC	38A
DORE	28E
Dormer Green LC	18A
Dorr Lane LC	40B
DOVERCOURT	9B
(Dowley Gap)	43
Down Enfield Viaduct	14B
DOWNHAM MARKET	12A
Dragonby Sidings	34B
Drax Power Station	40B
DRAYTON PARK	14A
DRIFFIELD	39B
Dringhouses North Jn	18B
Dringhouses North Jn	19
DRONFIELD	28E
Drove Road LC	13B
Drybeck Viaduct	45D
Dryclough Jn	41A, 43
Ducketts LC (R/G)	43
Dudding Hill Jn SB (DH)	1A
Dudley Bridleway LC	22B
DULLINGHAM	11C
DUNSTON	21B
DURHAM	20C
Durham Viaduct	20C
Durham Warping Drain Viaduct	33B
Dutch River Bridge Viaduct	40B
Duxford	11B
Eagle & Thorpe LC (AHBC-X)	27E
Eagle Barnsdale LC (AHBC)	27E
EAGLESCLIFFE	47C
Earfit Lane LC (R/G)	18B
Earsden	23C
Easby Viaduct	51B
Easington LC (FP)	23B
(Easington)	48B
EAST ANGLIAN RAILWAY MUSEUM	5E, 7B
East Bank Tunnel	28E
EAST BOLDON	49A
East Boldon LC (CCTV)	49A
East Cowick LC (R/G)	40B
East Cowton Crossovers	20B

(Marshland Jn)	33B
Marshmoor	15A
MARSKE	51A
Marston Hall No. 5 Gates LC (AHBC)	9A
Marston Moor LC (Gatebox)	42E
Martin Road LC	27A
Martins LC	12A
MARTON (formerly ORMESBY)	50B
Marton Carr LC (AOCL)	50B
Marton Lane LC (ABCL)	50B
MARYLAND	2B
Maryland East Crossovers	2B
Masborough Sorting Sdgs South Jn	29
Masborough Station Jn's	29
Masons LC	27B
Masserellas LC	18A
Matt Pitts Lane LC (AOCL-X)	26B
Maud Foster LC (AHBC)	26A
Maxey LC (CCTV)	16B, 24D
Maypole Rasen LC	28A
Mead Lane LC (FP) (R/G-X)	11A
Meadow Croft Farm LC	32B
Meadow Gates LC	39B
MEADOW WELL (Metro)	52
MEADOWHALL	29
MEADOWHALL INTERCHANGE (Supertram)	53
Meadows Exch. Sidings	24D
Meads Lane LC	18D
Meardsall LC	27E
Medge Hall LC (Gatebox)	33B
MELDRETH	24C
Meldreth Road LC (AHBC)	24C
Melkridge Siding	46C
Melling Tunnel	44C
Mellis LC (AHBC-X)	6D
MELTON (SUFFOLK)	9A
Melton Lane SB (ML) & LC (MG)	38B
MENSTON	43
Merrings LC	4B
METHERINGHAM	27A
Methley Jn	37A
Methley North LC	37A
Metro Tunnel	22A
METROCENTRE	21B
MEXBOROUGH	33A
Mexborough (East) Jn	33A
MICKLEFIELD	37B
Micklefield Jn	37B
Mickley LC (R/G)	21C
Middle Drove LC (R/G)	13C
Middlemere LC (AHBC)	12C
MIDDLESBROUGH	50A, 50B
Middleton LC (ABCL)	8
MIDDLETON PARK	37A
MIDDLETON RAILWAY TRUST LTD	37A
Middleton Towers LC (TMO)	12B
MIDDLEWOOD (Supertram)	53
Midland Jn (Dewsbury)	41B
MID-NORFOLK RAILWAY PRESERVATION TRUST	13B
Mile End (Devonshire Street)	2B
Mile End LC (Ely) (AHBC-X)	13A
Milford Jn & SB (M)	35B, 42B
Milford Sidings	35B
Milford West Sidings	37B
Mill Drove LC (AHBC-X)	12C
Mill Farm LC	39B
Mill Garth LC	18C
Mill Green SB (MG) & LC (MG)	26C
Mill Lane Jn SB (M)	43
Mill Race Jn	29
Millfield	47C
MILLFIELD (Metro)	48B
Millfield Farm LC	38A
Millmoor	29
Milne Viaduct	41A
Milner Road SB (MR)	41A
Milton Fen LC (AHBC)	11C
Milton Village LC (Gatebox)	46A
(Mineral Jn)	40B
Mineral Quay (Immingham) LC (TMO)	32B
Mingledale LC	39B
MIRFIELD	41A
Mirfield Viaduct	41A
MISTLEY	9B
Mistley LC (Footpath) (R/G)	9B
Mitre Bridge	1A
Moat Hills LC (CCTV)	17C, 18A
Molescroft Grange LC	39A
Molewood Tunnel	24A
Monk Bretton	39D
MONKSEATON (Metro)	52
Monkwearmouth Jn	48B
Monsanto LC (AOCL)	48A
Monsanto Siding Jn	48A
Monsanto/BASF LC (AOCL)	48A
MONUMENT (Metro)	52
Moody Lane LCs	32C
Moor Lane LC	34C
MOOR ROAD (LEEDS)	37A
Moorcock Tunnel	45B

Moorends Farm LC	33B
Moores LC	11C
MOORGATE (LUL)	14A
MOORTHORPE	33A, 35B, 36B
Moortown LC (AHBC-X)	28B
MORLEY	41B
Morley Tunnel	41B
MORPETH	22B
Mortimer Street Jn (former)	1A
Mortimer Street Viaduct	1A
Morton Grange Farm No. 4 LC	50B
Moss Cottages LC	46F
Moss LC	18A
Motts Lane LC (R/G-X)	5C
Moulton LC (AHBC-X)	6D
Mount Bures LC (ABCL)	5E
Mount Pleasant Farm LC	47C
Mountains LC	25C
Mountnessing Jn	10A
Mucking LC (AHBC)	4B
Munceys LC	12C
Museum GF (Chappel & Wakes Colne)	5E
Muskham Viaduct	16C
Muston LC (AHBC)	39C
MYTHOLMROYD	41A
Mytholmroyd Viaduct	41A
NAFFERTON	39B
Nafferton LC (AHBC-X)	39B
Nairns LC	11C
NATIONAL RAILWAY MUSEUM	19
Navarino Road Jn	1B, 10B
Naworth LC (AHBC-X)	46A
Naylors LC	24D
NEASDEN	1A
Neatherd Road LC (TMO)	13B
NEEB LC (Open)	48A
NEEDHAM MARKET	6C
Nene Carriage Sidings (Pet)	16A
NENE VALLEY RAILWAY	15D, 54A
Nether Lane LC (AHBC-X)	39B
Nether Poppleton LC (AHBC)	42E
NETHERFIELD	25A
Neville Hill Jns & Depot	37A
NEW BARNET	15A
New Barnetby LC	31C
New Bedford River Viaduct	13C
New Biggin	45C
NEW CLEE	32A
New Cut LC	18C
New England North Jn	16A
New England Sidings	16A
New Furnace Tunnel	43
New Ground Sidings	48A
NEW HOLLAND	32B
New House Farm LC	5D
New Inn LC (Immingham) (Open)	32B
New Kew Jn	1A
New Moor LC (AOCL)	23C
New Oak Farm LC	40B
NEW PUDSEY	43
New Pudsey Tunnel	43
New Sidings (Hull)	38C
NEW SOUTHGATE	14B
New Swinton Curve	33A
New York Farm LC	42D
NEWARK CASTLE	27D
Newark Crossing	16C, 27D
Newark Crossing East Jn	27D
Newark Crossing South Jn	27D
NEWARK NORTH GATE	16C
NEWCASTLE	22A
Newcombe's LC	18C
Newham LC (CCTV)	23A
Newham Road LC (TMO)	23C
NEWMARKET	11C
NEWPORT (Essex)	11B
Newport East Jn	49C, 50A
Newport Viaduct	11B
(Newport)	49C
Newsham Bates Staithes	23C
Newthorpe LC	37B
NEWTON AYCLIFFE	47B
Newton Flotman LC (AHBC-X)	6D
Newton Hall	20B, 21A
NEWTONDALE	51D
Niffany LC & Viaduct	44A
No. 2 LC (Brundall)	8
No. 6 LC (Ancaster)	25B
No. 12 LC (Beccles)	8
No. 13 LC (Beccles)	8
No. 18 LC (Rauceby)	25C
No. 18 LC (Sibsey)	26A
No. 22 LC (St. James Deeping)	26C
No. 23 LC (Acle)	8
No. 24 LC (St. James Deeping)	26C
No. 26 LC (Buckenham)	8
No. 29 LC (Great Coates)	32A
No. 30 LC (Buckenham)	8
No. 30 LC (Sibsey)	26A

No. 33 LC (Lakenheath)	13A
No. 43 Gate LC (Open)	4B
No. 53 LC (Lowestoft)	8
No. 54 LC (Lowestoft)	8
No. 56 LC (Lowestoft)	8
No. 58 LC (Lowestoft)	8
No. 59 LC (Lowestoft)	8
No. 65 Angels LC (Open) (R/G)	15C
No. 66 LC (FP) (R/G)	15C
No. 67 Cardells LC (Open) (R/G)	15C
No. 67 LC (Lowestoft)	8
No. 68 LC (Market Rasen)	28A
No. 71 LC (FP) (R/G)	15C
No. 72 LC (Lowestoft)	8
No. 76 LC (Lowestoft)	8
No. 79 LC (Spooner Row)	13B
No. 82 LC (Thirsk)	20A
No. 84 LC (Mill Green)	26C
No. 85 LC (Mill Green)	26C
No. 89 LC (Thirsk)	20A
No. 93 LC (Hartford Bridge)	13B
No. 135 LC (Blotoft)	26D
No. 150 LC (Alnmouth)	23A
No. 152 LC (Alnmouth)	23A
No. 155 LC (Alnmouth)	23A
No. 155 LC (CCTV) (Grays)	4B
No. 155A LC (Alnmouth)	23A
No. 158A LC(Alnmouth)	23A
No. 161 LC (Alnmouth)	23A
No. 162 LC (Alnmouth)	23A
No. 163 LC (Alnmouth)	23A
No. 167 LC(Alnmouth)	23A
No. 169 LC (Tweedmouth)	23A
No. 170 LC (Tweedmouth)	23A
No. 174 LC (R/G) (Tweedmouth)	23A
No. 176 LC (East Tilbury)	4B
No. 179 LC (R/G) (Tweedmouth)	23B
No. 193 LC (R/G) (Tweedmouth)	23B
No. 263 LC	18A
No. 316 LC (Saxilby)	27B
Noblethorpe LC	18A
Norden's Barn Farm LC	37B
Normanby Park GF	34B
NORMANTON	42A
Normanton LC (Bottesford) (AHBC-X)	25B
Norsk Hydro (Immingham)	32B
NORTH BAY RAILWAY (Scarborough)	19C
North Blyth	23C
North Carr LC	27C
North Cove LC	8
North Crossing LC (AOCL)	40B
North Drain Viaduct	26C
North Elmham	13B
North Fen LC (AHBC-X)	13C
North FLT (Felixstowe)	9A
North Gate LC	50B
North Green LC (AOCL)	8
North Jn	20B
North Kelsey LC (AHBC-X)	28B
North Lincoln Jn	34A
North London Line Viaduct	14A
NORTH NORFOLK RAILWAY	54B
North Pole Intl. Depot	1A
North Pole Jn	1A
North Quay Branch	9A
NORTH ROAD (Darlington)	20B, 47B
North Seaton LC (Gatebox)	23C
North Seaton Viaduct	23C
NORTH SHIELDS (Metro)	52
North Tees LC (AOCL)	48A
NORTH TYNESIDE STEAM RAILWAY	52
NORTH WALSHAM	8
North Western Ent. LC (Immingham)	32B
NORTH WOOLWICH	2C
NORTH YORKSHIRE MOORS RAILWAY	51D
North/South Access LC (Open)	48A
Northall Tunnel	20B
NORTHALLERTON	20B
Northfield Farm LC	20B
Northfleet Hope Terminal	4B
Northorpe LC SB (N)	31C
NORTHUMBERLAND PARK	10B
Norton East (Blackwells) LC	47C
Norton LC (Gatebox)	40A
Norton Parks LC	18C
Norton-on-Tees South SB (NS)	47C
Norton-on-Tees SB (N) & LC (MCB)	47C, 48A
Norton-on-Tees West LC (MCB)	47C
Norwell Lane LC (CCTV)	16C
NORWICH	7A
Norwich Road LC (AHBC-X)	8
Norwich Road LC (Mid. Norfolk) (TMO)	13B
Norwood Junction	21B
Norwood LC (Shirebrook)	30A
Norwood Road LC (AHBC)	13C
NOTTINGHAM	25A
Nottingham Branch Jn (Gran)	16C
Nottingham East & West Jns	25A
Nunnery Depot (Supertram)	53
Nunnery Jn	29

Staythorpe SB (SC) & LC (MCB)	27D
Steamtown	44C
STEETON & SILSDEN	44A
STEVENAGE	15B
(Stevenage Old Station)	15B
Stifford Viaduct	3B
(Stillington)	20C
Stilton Fen Emergency Crossovers	15D
Stocksbridge	29
STOCKSFIELD	21C
STOCKSMOOR	36A
Stocksmoor Jn	36A
STOCKTON	47C
Stoke Bridge LC (AOCL)	6B
Stoke Jn	16B
Stoke Lane LC (AHBC-X)	25A
STOKE NEWINGTON	10B
(Stoke SB)	16B
Stoke Summit/Tunnel	16B
Stokes Hall LC	10A
Stonea SB (S) & LC (MCG)	13C
Stonefield Farm No. 65 & 66 LC	28A
Stones Sidings LC	25C
Stora GSP	4A
Stourton	37A
Stow Bardolph LC (CCTV)	12B
Stow Park Tillbridge Lane SB (SP) & LC (MG)	27B
Stowgate LC (AHBC-X)	26C
Stowmaries LC	10A
STOWMARKET	6C
Stowmarket LC Gatebox	6C
Stranton SB	48A
STRATFORD	2B
STRATFORD INTERNATIONAL	2B
Stratford International East & West Jns	2B
STRATFORD LOW LEVEL	2B
Stratford Market Depot (LUL)	2B
Straws LC	12C
STREETHOUSE	39D
Streethouse LC (CCTV)	39D
Strensall SB (S) & LC (MCB)	19
Strumpshaw Fen LC	8
Strumpshaw LC	8
STRUMPSHAW OLD HALL STEAM	
MUSEUM RAILWAY	7D
Stubbs Walden North & South LC (CCTV)	40A
Sudbrook Lane LC (AHBC-X)	25B
SUDBURY (Suffolk)	5E
Sudforth Lane SB (S) & LC (MCB)	40A
Sugar Factory GF	38A
Summer Lane	36A
Sun Lane LC	43
Sun Wharf LC (AOCL)	9A
SUNDERLAND	48B
Sunderland North & South End Jns	48A
Sunderland South Dock	48B
Sunderland South Tunnel	48B
Sussex Street LC	50A
Suton LC (AHBC-X)	13B
Swaithe Viaduct	35D
Swallwell Jn	21B
Swan Fleet Lane LC	38A
Swanton Road LC (TMO)	13B
SWINDERBY	27E
Swinderby SB (S) & LC (MG)	27E
Swinderby Road LC (AHBC)	27E
Swinedyke LC (R/G)	31C
SWINESHEAD	25C
Swineshead LC (AHBC)	25C
Swing Bridge Jn	7A
Swingbridge Viaduct (Somerleyton)	8
SWINTON (S. Yorks)	33A
Switches Farm LC	44A
Syke Foot LC	45D
Sykes Lane LC	27B
Tabrums Cross LC	10A
Tallington Crossovers	16B
Tallington LC (CCTV)	16B
TANFIELD RAILWAY	47D
Tankersley Tunnel	29, 35D
Tapton Jn	28E
Tattershall Road LC (AHBC)	26A
Tatterthwaite LC	44B
Taylors LC	25B
Taylors LC	39C
Tees Bridge	47C, 49C
Tees Dock	50B
Tees No. 1 LC	49C
Tees SB (TY)	49C
Tees Works Siding	50B
Tees Yard	49C
TEES-SIDE AIRPORT	47C
Temple Hirst Jn	18A
(Temple Hirst)	18A
Temple Mills Depot & Control Room SB (CTRL)	10B
Temple Mills East & West Jns	2B, 10B
Temple Mills Lane	2B, 10B
Tempsford LC (CCTV)	15C

(Tempsford)	15C
Tennyson Avenue LC	12B
Terrace Sidings (Lincoln)	27A
Tetheringrass Lane LC	27B
Teversham LC (AHBC)	11C
Thackley Tunnels	43
Thames Board Mills LC	4A
Thames Haven	4B
(Thames Matex/Vopark)	4A
Tharston Viaduct	6D
THE BOWES RAILWAY CO LTD	49B
The Drove LC	13A
The Haggs LC	33B
The Poplars LC	47C
THEOBALDS GROVE	10B
THETFORD	13A
Third Drove LC (AHBC-X)	13C
THIRSK	20A
Thompsons LC	44A
Thompsons LC (R/G)	17B
Thonock Lane Farm LC	31C
Thoresby Cly	30A
Thoresby Colliery Jn SB	30A
THORNABY	49C
Thornaby East Jn	49C
Thornally No. 47 & 48 LCs	28A
Thorne Jn	33B
Thorne Lane LC	33B
Thorne Moorends LC (AHBC)	33B
Thorne No. 1 & 2 LCs (AHBC)	33B
THORNE NORTH	33B
Thorne Road LC (AHBC)	33B
THORNE SOUTH	33B
Thornfield House LC	40A
Thornhill Jn	41B
Thornhill LNW Jn	41B
Thornholme LC	39B
THORNTON ABBEY	32B
Thornton Fields Jn & Carriage Sdgs	2B
Thornton Gates LC	18C
THORPE BAY	3C
Thorpe Common LC	38A
THORPE CULVERT	26B
Thorpe Farm LC	38A
Thorpe Gates LC	37B
Thorpe Hall LC (RC)	37B
Thorpe Jn	7A
Thorpe Lane No. 3 Gates LC (AHBC)	9A
Thorpe LC (AOCL)	40A
Thorpe Salvin Bridleway LC	31A
Thorpe Yard (Norwich)	7A
THORPE-LE-SOKEN	6A
Thorpe-on-the-Hill LC (AHBC-X)	27E
Thorrington LC (MCG)	6A
(Three Counties)	15B
Three Gates LC	6A
Three Horse Shoes No. 1, 2 & 3 LCs	13C
Three Horse Shoes SB	13C
Thrislington Quarry	20C
Thrumpton SB (T)	17A, 31B
Thrumpton West Jn	31B
Thrybergh Jn	33A
THURGATON	25A
THURNSCOE	33A
THURSTON	12D
Thurston LC (Footpath) (R/G)	12D
Thurstonland Tunnel	36A
THUXTON	13B
Thuxton LC (TMO)	13B
Thwaite Gates LC (CCTV)	39A
Tickhill Viaduct	35A
Tilbury Dock	4B
(Tilbury East Jn)	4B
Tilbury Exchange Sidings	4B
Tilbury IRFT	4B
Tilbury Railport Jn (former Tilbury West Jn)	4B
Tilbury RCT	4B
TILBURY TOWN	4B
Tile Shed LC (AHBC-X)	49A
Tiled House Farm LC (AHBC)	12C
Tilehurst East Jn	5E
Tindall Bank LC	27C
TINSLEY YARD (former Main Yard)	29
Tinsleys (Campains Lane) LC	26C
Tinwell LC	24D
TI-Oxide Europe	32C
Tivetshall LC (AHBC-X)	6D
Tod Point Jn	50B
Tollerton	20A
Tolney Lane Viaduct	27D
Tomlinsons LC	27E
Tong Park Viaduct	43
Torworth LC (CCTV)	17B
Totley Tunnel East SB & Tunnel	28E
TOTTENHAM HALE	1B, 10B
Tottenham North Curve Tunnels	1A
Tottenham South Jn	1B, 10B
Tottenham West Jn	10B
TOWER GATEWAY	3A

Town End Farm LC	20B
Town Farm No. 1 & 2 LCs	39C
Transit Quays (Immingham)	32B
Trees LC (CCTV)	11B
Treeton Jn's	29
Treeton North Jn	29
Trent East Jn (Gains)	27B, 31B
Trent Fields Viaduct	25A
Trent Jn (Scunthorpe)	34A
Trent Lane LC (FP) (R/G)	25A
Trent Lane LC (Nottingham)	25A
Trent Sidings (Scunthorpe)	34A
Trent West Jn (Gains)	27B, 31B
TRIMLEY	9A
Trinity Lane LC	10B, 11A
Trowse	7A
Trowse Jn	7A
Trowse Lower Jn	7A
Trowse Swing Bridge	7A
Tunstans LC	47C
Tunstead Church Lane LC	8
Tunstead Market Street LC (AHBC)	8
TURKEY STREET	10B
Turner Street Footbridge	28E
Turners Lane Jn	42A
Tursdale Jn	20C
Tuxford	30B
Tuxford Emergency Crossovers	17A
Tweedmouth SB (TW) & Sidings	23B
Two Mile Bottom LC (AHBC-X)	13A
Tye Green Jn	11B
TYNE & WEAR METRO	52
Tyne Coal Terminal	49A
TYNE DOCK (Metro)	49A, 52
Tyne Dock Bottom	49A
Tyne Dock Loop	49A
Tyne Green LC	46E
Tyne Yard	21B
TYNEMOUTH (Metro)	52
Tyneside (IECC) (T)	22A
(Uffington & Barnack) LC (MGH)	24D
Uffington SB (UN)	24D
Ufford LC (ABCL)	9A
Ugley Lane LC	11B
ULCEBY	32B
Ulceby Chase Farm LC	32A
Ulceby North Jn	32B
Ulceby South Jn SB (UJ) & LC (MG)	32A, 32B
Ulgham Grange LC (CCTV)	22B
Ulgham Lane LC (CCTV)	22B
ULLESKELF	35C
UNIVERSITY (Metro)	48B
Unstone Viaduct	28E
Unthank LC (TMO)	47A
UPMINSTER	3B, 5B
UPMINSTER BRIDGE (LUL)	3B
UPNEY (LUL)	3A, 3B
Upney Jn	3A
Upper Denton LC (AHBC-X)	46B
Upper Denton West	46B
UPPER HOLLOWAY	1A, 1B
Upper Yard GF	46A
Upperby Bridge Jn	46A
Upperby Jn	46A
UPTON PARK (LUL)	3A
Urlay Nook SB (UN) & LC (MG)	47C
Usworth LC (former)	20C
Van Siding GF	48B
Vange Wharf LC (CCTV)	3B, 4B
Vaseys LC	20B
Viaduct Maintenance LC	11A
Victoria Line Depot (LUL)	10B
Victoria Park	1B
Victoria Road Covered Way	42D
Victoria Road LC (CCTV)	8
Victoria Road LC (Netherfield) (TOG)	25A
Victoria Sdgs (Norwich)	7A
Victoria Viaduct (Durham)	20C
Victoria Viaduct (Sheffield)	29
Villa Farm LC	18C
WADSLEY BRIDGE	29
Wadsley Viaduct	29
WAINFLEET	26B
Wakefield Europort	42A
WAKEFIELD KIRKGATE	42A
Wakefield Kirkgate West Jn	36C, 42A
Wakefield Road Tunnel	43
WAKEFIELD WESTGATE	36C
Waldersea LC (TMO)	13C
Walesby LC (AHBC-X)	28A
WALKERGATE (Metro)	22A, 52
Walkeringham LC	27B
Walkeringham Misterton	27B
Walkers LC	20B, 27E
Wallgate LC	18C
WALLSEND (Metro)	52
Walpole LC (CCTV)	8

ENGINEERS LINE REFERENCES

The boundary of each ELR is indicated by the page references. Where both boundaries appear on the same page, only one reference is given. Where one appears in another Track Diagram, the reference is in the format Book:page

ABE	Allington West Jn. - Barkston East Jn.	25B
ACD	Allington Chord	25B
ACW	Acton Canal Wharf - Willesden	1A
ADH	Alexandra Dock - Hessle Road Jn. (Hull)	38C
ANL	Acton - Northolt Line (via Greenford East)	1A, 3:19A
ATG	Turnham Green (LUL) - Gunnersbury Jn.	1A, 5:44A
AWL	Acton East - Acton Wells Jn.	1A, 3:1B
AWP	Anlaby Road Jn. - West Parade North Jn. (Hull)	38C
BCB	Black Carr Jn. - Bessacarr Jn.	17C
BCE	Bolsover Colliery Empties	30A
BDH	Brent Curve Jn. - Dudding Hill Jn.	1A
BDM	Bow Depot Midland	2B
BEC	Bevercotes Colliery	30B
BEW	Beighton Jn. - Woodhouse Jn.	29
BGE	Boldon Colliery Jn. - Green Lane Jn.	49A
BGK	Bethnal Green - Kings Lynn	2A, 12A
BHM	Barrow Roundhouse Railway Centre	28E
BHP	Boultham Jn. - Pyewipe Jn.	27A
BIB	Shipley West Jn. - Bradford Jn.	43
BKS	Brancliffe East Jn. - Kirk Sandall Jn.	35A, 33B
BLJ	Shepcote Lane East Jn. - Broughton Lane Jn.	29
BNE	Benton North Jn. - Earsdon Jn.	23C
BNW	Boldon New Curve : Boldon East Jn. - Boldon North Jn.	49A
BNY	Green Lane Jn. - Dean Road Sidings	49A
BOC	Bolsover Colliery (Seymour Jn. - Bolsover)	30A
BOH	Bowesfield Jn. - Hartburn Jn.	47C
BOK	Broad Street - Old Kew Jn. (North London Line)	1B, 1A
BOO	Bowers Row Opencast (Castleford)	42A
BRA	Braintree Branch (Witham - Braintree)	5D
BRI	Brocklesby Jn. - Immingham Dock	32A, 32B
BTB	Barlow Tip Branch	18A
BTE	Barking Tilbury Line Jn. East - Barking East Jn. - Upney Jn. (Connecting line)	3A
BTJ	Brightside - Treeton Jn. (Tinsley Yard)	29
BWC	Bedlington Jn. - Woodhorn Colliery	23C
BWO	Ashington Jn. - Butterwell Jn. (Butterwell Disposal Point)	23C, 22B
BWT	Barking Tilbury Line Jn. - Barking Tilbury Line Jn. West	3A
BYE	Bury St. Edmunds Yard	12D
CAW	Cricklewood Curve Jn. - Acton Wells Jn.	1A
CBC	Carnforth North Jn. - Carlisle South Jn. via Whitehaven	44C, 46A
CBE	Cambridge Goods	11C
CCB	Rectory Jn. - Cotgrave Colliery	25A
CCH	Cambridge (Coldham Lane Jn.) - Haughley Jn.	11C, 12D
CCN	Clipstone Colliery North (Rufford Jn. - Clipstone Colliery)	30A
CDY	Chelmsford Lower Yard	5C
CEC	Carnforth East Jn. - Carnforth Station Jn.	44C
CER	Colchester Goods	6A
CFM	Church Fenton North Jn. - Micklefield Jn.	35C, 37B
CFP	Canonbury West Jn. - Finsbury Park	1B, 14A
CGJ	Crewe - Carlisle	46A, 4:13
CHM	Channelsea North Jn. - High Meads Jn.	2B
CHR	Chesterfield (Tapton Jn.) - Rotherham Masborough Stn N. Jn. (Old Road)	28E, 29
CHS	Crigglestone Jn. - Horbury Jn.	36A
CJC	Clapton Jn. - Chingford	10B
CJS	Carcroft - Stainforth Jn.	36B, 33B
CNS	Carpenters Road North - Carpenters Road South	2B
COC	Colchester - Clacton	6A
CPM	Castleford West Jn. - Pontefract West Jn.	39D
CPS	Cottam Power Station	31B
CRC	Camden Road Jn. - Camden Jn.	1A
CRF	Camden Road Central Jn. - Copenhagen Jn.	1A, 14A
CRS	Cromer - Sheringham	8
CST	Carpenters Road North - Stratford Central Jn. West	2B
CTH	Colne Jn. - Hythe Jn.	6A
CTL	Calder Bridge Jn. - Turners Lane Jn.	42A
CTP	Connington Tip Siding	15D
CWJ	Camden Jn. - Watford Jn. (DC lines)	1A
CWS	Clipstone West Jn. - Clipstone South Jn.	30A
DAE	Darlington, Parkgate Jn. - Eastgate-in-Weardale	20B, 47A
DDY	Doncaster Down Side Yards	17C
DEX	Derby Extension : Colwick and Gedling Colliery	25A
DJH	Daisyfield Jn. - Hellifield South Jn.	44B
DOC	Kings Lynn Dock	12B
DOL	Doncaster, Marshgate Jn. - Leeds	17C, 37A
DOW	Doncaster - Wrawby Jn.	17C, 34C
DRA	Drax Power Station	40B
DRS	Dewsbury East Jn. - Dewsbury Railway Street	41B
DSN	Darlington - Saltburn	20B, 51A
DUY	Doncaster Up Side Yards	17C
DWS	Dore West Jn. - Dore Station Jn.	28E
DWW	Dalston Western Jn. - North Woolwich	1A, 2C

ECM	East Coast Main Line : London, Kings Cross - Edinburgh	14A, 1:11A
EDE	Eden Valley Line : Warcop - Appleby North Jn.	45C
EGG	Eggborough Power Station	40A
EJM	Earsdon Jn. - Morpeth North Jn.	23C, 22B
ELN	Engine Shed Jn. - Leeds West Jn.	37A
EMP	Ely North Jn. - March - Peterborough : Crescent Jn.	12A, 16A
ENT	Enfield Town Branch : Bury St Jn. - Enfield Town	10B
ESK	East Suffolk : Ipswich - Oulton Broad North Jn.	6C, 8
ETN	Ely North Jn. - Thetford - Norwich : Trowse Lower Jn.	12A, 7A
EWC	Ely West Curve : Ely North Jn. - Ely West Jn.	12A
FAS	Fletton Ash Sidings (Peterborough)	15D
FED	Felixstowe Dock : Trimley - Felixstowe Dock via N. Freightliner Terminal	9A
FEL	Felixstowe Beach : Westerfield Jn. - Felixstowe	9A
FEP	Ferryhill (Leamside Line) - Pelaw	20C, 49A
FGW	Forest Gate Jn. - Woodgrange Park	5A
FKW	Ferrybridge North Jn. - Knottingley West Jn.	35B, 40A
FOM	Fletton Jn. - Orton Mere	15D
FRC	Frickley Colliery Branch (Closed)	33A
FSS	London, Fenchurch Street - Shoeburyness	3A, 3C
FWR	Flyover West Jn. - Rossington Colliery	17C
GCD	Great Chesterford Siding	11B
GDL	Goole Docks Line	40B
GFB	Gas Factory Jn. - Bow Jn.	2B
GLT	Green Lane - Tyne Dock	49A
GMS	Grantham Sidings	16C
GOJ	Gospel Oak Jn. - Junction Road Jn.	1A
GRD	Greetland Jn. - Dryclough Jn.	41A
GRE	Graham Road Curve (Hackney)	1B
GRS	Grantham : former Barkston East Jn. - Skegness	25B, 26A
GRW	Griffen Wharf (Ipswich)	6B
GSM	Kettering North Jn. - Nottingham via Melton	24D
GUE	Esholt Jn. - Dockfield Jn. (Shipley)	43
HAC	Harworth Colliery : Firbeck Jn. - Harworth	35A
HAH	Haverton Hill South Branch : Belasis Lane Jn. - Haverton Hill South	48A
HAU	Habrough Jn. - Ulceby South Jn.	32A
HAY	Harrogate - York	42D, 19
HBS	Hull - Bridlington - Seamer	38C, 18D
HCD	Holmes Chord/Curve (Rotherham)	29
HCS	Heaton Carriage Sidings	22A
HDB	Hertford North Loop : Alexandra Palace - Hertford North - Langley South Jn.	14B, 24D
HDT	Hackney Downs Jn. - Cheshunt Jn.	10B, 11A
HEB	Hertford East Branch : Broxbourne Jn. - Hertford East	11A
HIM	Shirebrook East Jn. - High Marnham	30A, 30B
HJB	Hexthorpe Jn. - Bentley Jn. (Doncaster Avoiding Line)	33A
HJM	Hepscott Jn. - Morpeth Jn.	22B
HJS	Hessle Road Jn. - Saltend	38C
HLD	Hartlepool Docks	48A
HLF	Hall Lane Jn. - Foxlow Jn.	28E
HLK	High Level Bridge Jn. - King Edward Bridge South Jn.	22A
HMC	Hatfield Main Colliery (Stainforth)	33B
HNB	Hendon Branch : Ryhope Grange Jn. - Sunderland South Dock	48B
HNC	Hambleton North Curve	18B
HOS	Holgate Jn. - Skelton Jn. via Slow lines	19
HOU	Barnes Jn. - Feltham Jn. via Hounslow (Hounslow Loop)	1A
HPC	Hare Park Jn. - Crofton West Jn.	36C, 39D
HPQ	Harwich, Parkeston Yard	9B
HPW	Harringay Park Jn. - Harringay Jn.	1B, 14A
HSC	Hambleton South Curve	18B
HUE	Hunslet East Goods (Leeds)	37A
HUL	Hull - Leeds	38C, 37A
HYM	Healey Mills Yard (Wakefield)	41B
ICS	Ilford Car Sheds	5A
ILK	Apperley Jn. - Ilkley	43
INW	Immingham Dock North West Entrance	32B
IPD	Ipswich Dock : Ipswich Upper Yard - Freight Terminal etc	6B
ISC	Isabella Colliery (Newsham North Jn. - Newsham Bates)	23C
IUP	Ipswich Upper Yard	6C
JAW	Pelaw Jn. - Jarrow Oil Terminal	49A
JCA	Joan Croft Jn. - Applehurst Jn.	18A, 33B
JMM	Ferrybridge Power Station	35B
JRT	Junction Road Jn. - Carlton Road.Jn. (Tottenham Lines)	1A
KBF	Kelloe Bank Foot (Ferryhill)	20C
KEB	King Edward Bridge East Jn. - North Jn.	22A
KES	Knottingley East Jn. - Knottingley South Jn.	40A
KGC	Kensal Green Jn. - Willesden Jn. (City lines)	1A
KGD	King George Dock (Hull)	38C
KGW	Kensal Green Jn. - Willesden LL	1A
KIL	Killingholme Branch : Immingham West Jn. - Killingholme	32B
KWS	Knottingley West Jn. - Shaftholme Jn.	40A

Code	Description	Ref
LBE	Leeds. Holbeck Jn. - Bradford Interchange	37A, 43
LCJ	Loversall Jn. - Flyover East Jn.	17C
LCR	Loversall Carr Jn. - Rossington Colliery Jn.	17C
LEC	London, Euston - Crewe	1A
LEH	Leeds, Armley Jn. - Harrogate	37A, 42B
LEN	Leeds - Newcastle East Jn. via Hartlepool (part closed)	37A, 22A
LLG	Willesden, West London Jn. - Sudbury Jn. (Low Level Lines)	1A
LLP	Longlands Loop Jn. - Boroughbridge Jn.	20B
LLS	Lea Jn. - Temple Mills East Jn.	2B
LTN	London, Liverpool Street - Norwich via Ipswich	2A, 7A
MAC	Deepcar - Cleethorpes (Manchester - Cleethorpes)	29
MAH	Manningtree - Harwich Town	6A, 9B
MAM	Maltby Colliery Branch Jn. - Maltby Colliery	35A
MAS	Dore South Jn. - Chinley North Jn. (Manchester and Sheffield Mid)	28E
MBW	Middlesbrough - Whitby	50B, 51C
MCG	Carlisle, Currock Jn. - (Forks Jn.) - Rome Street Jn.	46A
MCL	London, Moorgate - Carlton Road Jn. (Midland City Line)	1A
MDL	Thornhill LNW Jn. - Copley Hill East Jn. (Manchester - Diggle - Leeds) (See MVL)	41B, 37A
MEB	Moorgate Branch : London, Moorgate - Finsbury Park	14A
MEW	Methley Jn. - Whitwood Jn.	37A, 42A
MGW	Milford Jn. - Gascoigne Wood Jn.	35B, 37B
MIT	Middleton Towers Branch : Kings Lynn Jn. - Middleton Towers	12B
MKB	Monk Bretton Branch	39D
MLN	Paddington - Penzance via Bristol (Main Line)	1A
MMC	Markham Main Colliery : Markham Sidings - Markham Main Colliery	17C
MRB	Milner Royd Jn. - Bradford Interchange	41A, 43B
MUP	March Up and Down Yards	13C
MVL	Diggle Jn. - Heaton Lodge Jns. (Manchester Victoria - Leeds) (See MDL)	4:45C, 41A
MVN	Manchester Victoria - Normanton, Goose Hill Jn.	41A, 42A
MWJ	Marchey House Jn. - Winning Colliery Jn.	23C
MWL	March West Jn. - March Whitemoor Jn.	13C
MWN	Marsh West Jn. - Grimsby Docks	32A, 32C
NAJ	Neasden South Jn. - Aynho Jn.	1A, 3:13B
NAY	Brundall Jn. - Great Yarmouth	8
NCW	Norwich, Wensum Curve	7A
NEC	Newcastle, King Edward Bridge South Jn. - Blaydon Jn. - Carlisle South Jn.	22A, 46A
NEN	Newburn Branch : Newcastle West Jn. - Forth Banks	22A
NGC	Netherfield Jn. - Colwick North Jn.	25A
NGD	Carlisle, London Road Jn. - Bog Jn. (Newcastle Goods lines)	46A
NHM	Neville Hill Depot and Sidings	37A, 43A
NJN	Neasden Curve : Neasden Jn. - Neasden South Jn.	1A
NKE	New Kew Jn. - Kew East Jn.	1A
NLF	Norwood Jn. - Low Fell	21B
NOB	Nottingham East Junction - Barnetby	25A, 31B
NOC	Normanton, Altofts Jn. - Colton Jn.	42A, 35C
NOE	North Elmham Branch : Wymondham - North Elmham	13B
NOG	Nottingham - Grantham	25A, 16C
NOL	Norwich - Oulton Broad - Lowestoft	7A, 8
NOP	Normanby Park Branch (formerly Scunthorpe West Jn. - Normanby Park)	34A
NSE	Newark Crossing South Jn. - Newark Crossing East Jn.	16C, 27C
NTE	Manningtree North Jn. - East Jn.	6A
NUJ	Nunnery Main Line Jn. - Nunnery Jn.	29
NWE	Norton-on-Tees West Jn. - Norton-on-Tees East Jn.	47C
OAJ	Oakenshaw South Jn. - Oakenshaw Jn.	39D
OSC	Oakenshaw South Jn. - Crofton East Jn.	39D
OXO	Oxcroft Opencast : Oxcroft Jn. - Oxcroft Opencast	30A
PBS	Pye Bridge Jn. - Shireoaks East Jn. (South section)	4:5, 30A
PED	Penistone - Doncaster	36A, 17C
PEF	Pontefract, East Jn. - Ferrybridge South Jn.	40A
PEH	Penistone - Huddersfield	36A
PGS	Palace Gates	14B
PHC	Hull Yard - Dairycoates	38B
PHS	Peterborough Sidings	16A
PLG	Park Lane Jn. - Greensfield Jn.	22A
PMJ	Peterborough - Manton Jn.	16A, 24D
POC	Billingham Jn. - Port Clarence	48A
PSE	Pye Bridge Jn. - Shireoaks East Jn. (North section)	30A, 31A
PYE	Pyewipe: Immingham East Dock Jn. - Grimsby Docks	32B, 32C
RBY	Reedham - Berney Arms - Great Yarmouth	8
RDG	London, Waterloo (Windsor lines) - Reading via Richmond	1A, 5:27A
REB	Northallerton, Castle Hills Jn. - Redmire	20B, 45E
RLY	Ripple Lane Yards	4A
ROU	Romford - Upminster	5B
RUB	Rufford Colliery Jn. - Bilsthorpe Colliery	30A
RUC	Rufford Colliery Jn. - Rufford Colliery	30A
SAC	Settle Jn. – Carlisle, Petteril Bridge Jn.	45A, 46A
SAN	Santon Ore Branch (Scunthorpe)	34A
SAR	South Acton Jn. - Richmond	1A
SBF	Shipley East Jn. - Bradford Forster Square	43
SBR	Shepreth Branch : Hitchin, Cambridge Jn. - Shepreth Branch Jn.	15B, 11C
SCD	Scunthorpe, Trent Jn. - Dawes Lane Jn.	34A
SCG	Carlisle, Bog Jn. - Forks Jn.	46A
SCW	Scarborough, Gallows Close Goods	18D
SDC	Stratford Central Jn. West - Copper Mill North Jn.	2B, 10B
SEA	Dawdon Jn. - Seaham Harbour	48B
SEC	Selby Canal Jn. - Selby West Jn.	38A
SEL	Shepcote Lane West Jn. - Tinsley South Jn.	29
SES	Seal Sands Branch (North Tees)	48A
SEY	Seymour Colliery Branch (Barrow Hill)	30A
SHB	Sheffield : Wincobank Jn. - Barnsley : Quarry Jn	29, 36A
SHG	Sherburn Jn. - Gascoigne Wood Jn.	35C
SHU	Shoeburyness Sidings	3C
SHW	Shireoaks West Jn. - Woodend Jn.	31A
SIZ	Sizewell Sidings (Saxmundham - Leiston)	9A
SJB	St. James Jn. - Bridge Jn. (Doncaster)	17C
SJC	Carnforth, former Furness & Midland Jn. - former Wennington Jn.	44C
SJM	Swinton Jn. - Mexborough	33A
SKA	Skellow Jn. - Adwick Jn.	36B
SKL	Stocksbridge Light Railway	29
SKM	South Kirkby Jn. - Moorthorpe Station Jn.	35B
SKS	Skipton Middle Jn.- Grassington	44A
SKW	Skipton North Jn. - former Wennington Jn.	44A, 44C
SMJ	Swinton Jn. - Milford Jn.	33A, 35B
SNW	Sleaford North Jn. - West Jn.	25C
SOB	Soham Branch (Chippenham Jn. - Ely Dock Jn.)	12D, 12C
SOT	Seaton-on-Tees Branch : Seaton Snook Jn. - Seaton-on-Tees	48A
SPC	London, St. Pancras - Chesterfield, Tapton Jn. (former Midland Rly)	4:1R, 28E
SPD	Spalding South Jn. - Doncaster, Decoy North Jn.	26C, 17C
SPW	Springbank North Jn. - Walton Street Jn.	38C
SSE	Sleaford South Jn. - East Jn.	25C
SSH	Scunthorpe Yards	34A
SSK	Saltburn West Jn. - Skinningrove	51A
SSL	Seven Sisters Loop : South Tottenham West Jn. - Seven Sisters Jn.	10B
SSV	Shenfield - Southend Victoria	5B, 10A
STB	St. Botolph's Branch : East Gate Jn. - Colchester Town (St. Botolph's)	6A
STF	Norton South Jn. - Ferryhill South Jn. (Stillington - Ferryhill)	47C
SUD	Sudbury Branch : Marks Tey - Sudbury	5E
SWP	Shirebrook Jn. - Warsop Jn.	30
TAH	Junction Road Jn. - Barking (Tottenham and Hampstead)	1A, 3A
TCW	Temple Hirst Jn. - Selby South Jn. (Temple Hirst - Chaloner Whin.)	18A, 38A
TDE	Tilbury Docks East Side (Grays East Jn. - Northfleet Hope)	4B
TEN	Stansted East - North Loop	11B
TEY	Tyne Yard	21B
TFC	Thornton Fields Carriage Sidings	2B
THG	Thorpe Goods (Norwich)	7A
THN	Thames Haven Branch	4B
TJC	Chesterfield, Tapton Jn. - Old Skipton North Jn. (for Colne) (former Midland Rly)	28E, 44A
TJG	Thorne Jn. - Gilberdyke	33B, 40C
TLA	Stansted Airport Link (Third London Airport)	11B
TLL	Tilbury Loop Line : Barking, Tilbury Line Jn. East - Pitsea Jn. via Tilbury	3A, 4B
TNC	Treeton North Jn. - Catcliffe Jn. (Closed)	29
TSE	South Tottenham East Jn. - Tottenham South Jn.	10B
TSN	Trent South Jn. - Nottingham East Jn.	4:6A, 25A
TSY	Tees Yard	49C
TWN	Thorpe-le-Soken - Walton-on-the-Naze	6A
TYB	Clarborough Jn. - Cottam Power Station (Torksey Branch)	31B
TYC	Thoresby Colliery : Thoresby Colliery Jn. - Thoresby Colliery	30A
UCJ	Carlisle, Upperby Jn. - Caldew Jn. (Goods Lines)	46A, 4:29C
UDS	Doncaster, Low Ellers Curve Jn - Potteric Carr Jn.	17C
UHL	Willesden : Up & Down High Level Goods	1A
UPG	Upminster - Grays	3B, 4B
WAG	Wakefield - Goole	42A, 40B
WAR	Appleby North Jn. - Appleby West Jn.	45C
WAW	Willesden, Low Level Goods Jn. - Acton Wells Jn.	1A
WBC	West Burton Power Station	31B
WBH	Westgate Branch (Rotherham)	29
WCI	Wilton Branch (Teesside)	50B
WCM	Carlisle - Glasgow Central (West Coast Main Line)	46A, 4:29C
WEB	Werrington Branch : Werrington Jn. - Spalding	16A, 26C
WHC	Whitlingham Jn. - Cromer	7A, 8
WHR	Whiskerhill Jn. (Thrumpton West Jns.) - Retford Western Jn.	31B, 17A
WIG	Wisbech Goods Branch : March, Whitemoor Jn. - Wisbech	13C
WIS	Wickford - Southminster	10A
WKC	Welbeck Colliery Branch : Welbeck Colliery Branch Jn. - Welbeck Colliery	30A
WLL	Clapham Jn, Falcon Jn. - Willesden, West London Jn. (West London Line)	1A
WMB	Willesden High Level Jn. - Mitre Bridge Jn.	1A
WME	Woodburn Jn. - Mexborough Jn.	29, 33A
WRG	Whitehall Road Goods (Leeds)	37A
WSB	West Sleekburn Jn. - North Blyth	23C
WTB	West Blythe Staithes : Blythe Staithes Jn. - West Blythe Staithes	23C
WWK	Wakefield Westgate South Jn. - Wakefield Kirkgate West Jn.	42A
WZS	Willesden TMD	1A
YDS	St. Catherines Jn. - Decoy South Jn. (Doncaster)	17C
YMS	York - Malton - Scarborough	19, 18D

Notes